CW01237065

RICE

Text © 2025 Makiko Sano

Photography © 2025 Simon Smith

Published by OH
An Imprint of HEADLINE PUBLISHING GROUP LIMITED

1

Apart from any use permitted under UK copyright law, this publication may only be reproduced, stored, or transmitted, in any form, or by any means, with prior permission in writing of the publishers or, in the case of reprographic production, in accordance with the terms of licences issued by the Copyright Licensing Agency.

Cataloguing in Publication Data is available from the British Library

ISBN 978-1-03542-445-0

Printed and bound in China by Toppan Leefung Printing Ltd.

Headline's policy is to use papers that are natural, renewable and recyclable products and made from wood grown in well-managed forests and other controlled sources. The logging and manufacturing processes are expected to conform to the environmental regulations of the country of origin.

Editorial: Heather Boisseau / Matt Tomlinson
Design: James Pople
Production: Rachel Burgess
Picture Research: Paul Langan

HEADLINE PUBLISHING GROUP LIMITED
An Hachette UK Company
Carmelite House
50 Victoria Embankment,
London EC4Y 0DZ

The authorised representative in the EEA is Hachette Ireland
8 Castlecourt Centre
Dublin 15, D15 XTP3, Ireland (email: info@hbgi.ie)

www.headline.co.uk
www.hachette.co.uk

RICE

80 EASY RICE RECIPES
FROM MOCHI AND MISO TO SUSHI AND SAKE

MAKIKO SANO

(OH)

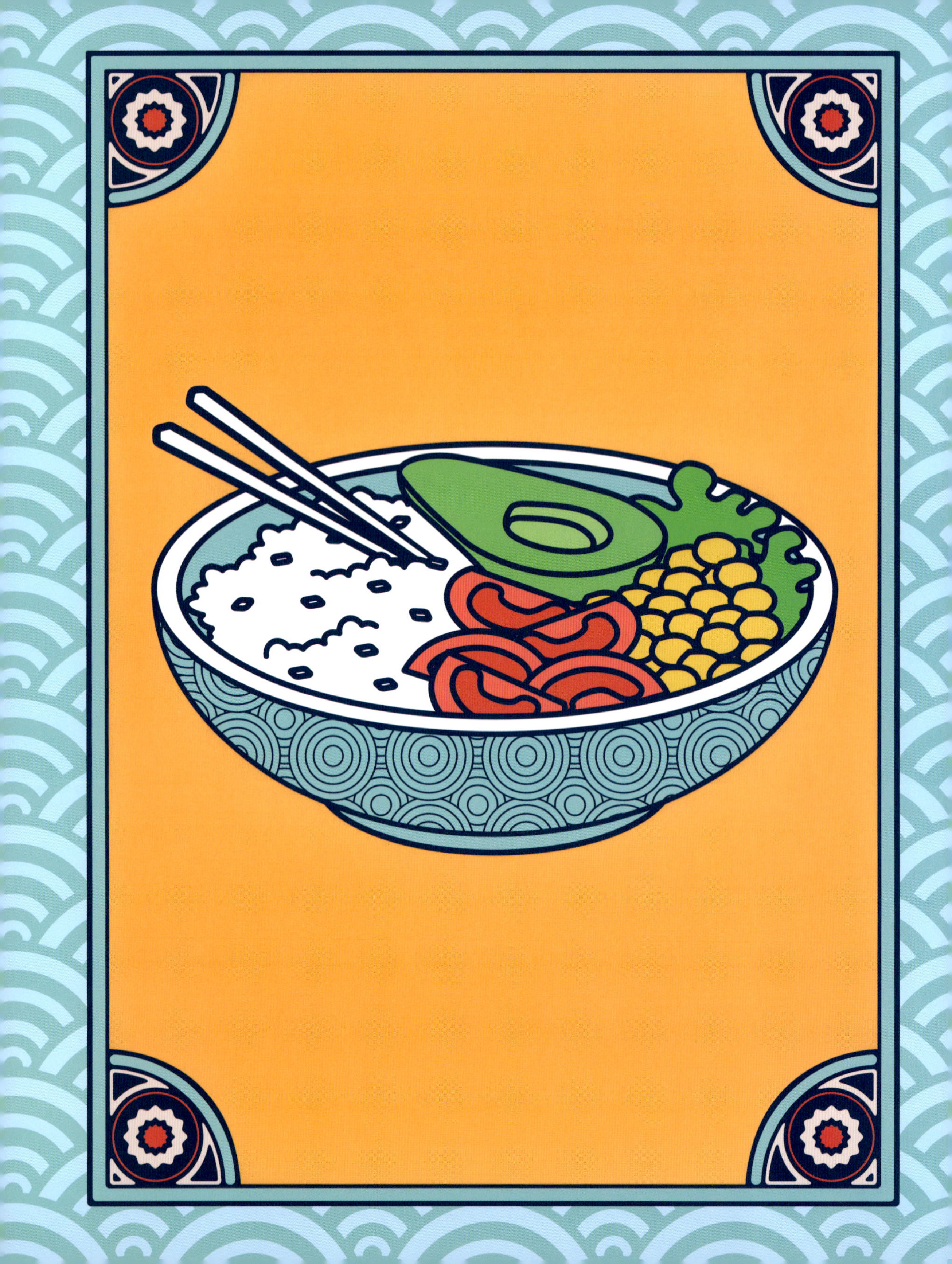

CONTENTS

THE CULTURE OF RICE IN JAPAN	6
RICE FAMILIES	10
HOW TO COOK PERFECT RICE EVERY TIME	14

KAKE GOHAN	**19**
DONBURI	**31**
RICE NOODLES	**49**
ONIGIRI, BREAKFASTS & MORE	**65**
RICE COOKER DISHES	**87**
RICE FLOUR	**103**
FRIED RICE	**121**
TAKIKOMI GOHAN HOTATE	**139**
RICE PAPER	**151**

INDEX	170
INGREDIENTS & SUPPLIERS	174
ABOUT THE AUTHOR	176
CREDITS	176

THE CULTURE OF RICE IN JAPAN

To understand how important rice is to Japanese culture, you just need to look at how entwined it is with the Japanese language. The ancient name of Japan was *Mizuho-no-kuni*, which endearingly translates as 'land of the water stalk plant' – in other words, rice. In fact, Japanese contains more words for rice than for love, and the word *gohan* not only refers to cooked rice but is also the word for meal, underscoring just how integral these pearly grains are.

In Japan, rice is a symbol of blessing, abundance, good health and joy. It is a revered ingredient, which makes our Western views of rice, or lack thereof, pale in comparison. We rather overlook our most commonly consumed, fairly standard, long grain or basmati varieties. Learning more about the traditions and history of rice bestows a new respect upon this simple ingredient and opens myriad creative possibilities to cook with and enjoy this starchy cereal grain.

Rice has been a staple food and cultural icon in Japan for centuries. It is thought that rice first came to Japan from China, via Korea, around 400 BCE, although great efforts were made to distinguish Japanese rice and the whole identity of Japan from other Asian neighbours. Japanese rice became known as the silver rice, marking it out from any imported varieties.

By the seventh century, rice was perceived as such a valuable commodity in Japan that it was traded as payment from land workers to their landlords. The first emperor of Japan was a farmer and 'priest king', who had exceptional abilities to communicate with the gods to ensure a good rice harvest. Various mythologies tell of the emperor descending from the sun goddess, who sent him on his way to Earth with her precious rice grains. His mission was to fill the land with abundant crisp, green stalks of rice plants. Many of his priestly functions revolved around rice-growing, and the tradition has continued into recent times, with Emperor Hirohito (1901–1989) tending to a rice plot in the Imperial Palace grounds in Tokyo into old age. Many Imperial rituals still centre around rice and the Japanese reverence of this food staple.

Rice is also a symbol of wealth, prosperity and purity, and it has played a vital role in shaping the country's culinary traditions and societal practices. Shinto followers, who believe in nature deities, offer sake (rice wine) and rice to the gods and their ancestors. In Hiroshima prefecture, rice-planting rituals still continue: cattle are decorated with necklaces, and the women of the village sing as they transplant the new rice seedlings to the paddy fields, levelled with an *eburi*, a tool said to contain the deity of rice fields. At ceremonial events and weddings, red rice known as *okowa* – comprising steamed adzuki beans, cowpeas and glutinous rice – is traditionally served, and *mochi* – Japanese rice cakes – are a New Year must for households throughout Japan.

Rice growing has shaped the landscape and traditions of rural Japan. Japanese social interaction is in part down to the traditional ways of cultivating rice in the fields. Communities worked patiently and politely together to seed, tend and harvest the important grain. Because of the labour-intensive process,

Opposite: A 1770 illustration showing the making of rice cakes.
Above: A rice-planting ritual in Kitahiroshima, Japan.

THE CULTURE OF RICE IN JAPAN

families would join neighbours to combine forces. To ensure that the rice harvest was a success required a group effort and a spirit of harmony and cooperation. This idea of community is even evident in the manner in which sake is enjoyed in Japan. You must fill the glass of another, with people taking turns to fill each other's glass but never their own.

While we might think of the pristine white colour of sushi rice as synonymous with Japanese rice, brown rice was historically the most widely consumed variety. No wonder, as it required less processing. White rice, which was far more labour intensive and therefore more expensive to produce, was only accessible to wealthier classes.

Today, rice cultivation spans across all regions of Japan, from Hokkaido to Okinawa. The different rice-growing regions of Japan each produce their own unique-tasting grains. The flavour signature differs depending on local climate and geography, and there are thought to be 300 varieties of Japanese rice.

Japanese meals nearly always incorporate rice alongside multiple other dishes, and are referred to as *ichi-juu san-sai*, or "one soup, three sides". Usually, these meals combine dishes of flavoured or plain rice, protein bowls of fish and tofu, and vegetables or pickles along with a soup, invariably miso. It is always a balanced selection. Modern influences in cooking, easy-prepare rice cookers and our changing lifestyles have seen the rise of rice dishes that combine the different elements in one bowl. Curry Doria, for example, is a rice gratin topped with cheese – a much more recent addition to what was previously a nearly dairy-free diet. TikTok is filled with *omurice* clips, showing beautifully crafted omelettes being draped over a dome of rice then slit open to ooze over the rice. And, beyond snacks, sake, desserts and miso, rice is even making its way into skincare products.

In this book you will find a host of recipes that work beautifully as a main meal or can be set alongside an array of smaller dishes, along with condiments to dress your rice and fail-safe guides to cooking and preparing perfect rice every time.

> **'Mokarimakka?'** is a common greeting in Osaka. It translates as, 'Are you making good money?' This may sound oddly forward, but it has its roots in a traditional Nepalese greeting used between rice-field workers, to enquire how much rice they had harvested that day.

Left: An example of an *ichi-juu san-sai* meal.
Opposite: Sake barrels stacked in Tokyo, Japan.

商標
芳醇清酒
十一正宗
大吟醸
森戸酒造
登録 商標
小林酒造株式会社
商標
越後国酒
登録 商標
柏露
越後長岡銘酒
柏露酒造
登録 商標
菊水
長生自得
千年寿
菊水酒造株式会社
商標
鈴鹿蔵元
鈴鹿川
スズカガワ
味酒鈴鹿国
ウマサケスズカノクニ
清水清三郎商店
登録 商標
噴井
ふきい
清酒
石川酒造
登録商標
清酒
登録 商標
芳醇清酒
登録 商標
酒 王
和楽
千秋寿

RICE FAMILIES

There are three main types of rice:

Japonica Short, roundish, glossy grains which are the stickiest and clingiest when cooked. Produced in Japan, Korea, China and parts of Europe and used for all types of Japanese and Asian cuisine.

Indica A long, slender-grained rice, produced mainly in central and southern China, Thailand, India and the US, and the most familiar in Western cuisine.

Javanica A mix of japonica and indica cultivated in sub-tropical regions like Southeast Asia, Italy and Spain. Its broad, thick grains are used for dishes like paella and risotto.

KNOW YOUR JAPANESE RICE

We think of rice as a fairly generic food stuff, with perhaps two or three varieties, but in Japan it has an almost cult status and underpins nearly every signature Japanese dish, from the ancient grains of purple rice to the comforting squish of sticky rice.

The most commonly eaten Japanese rice types fall into two categories: glutinous and non-glutinous. Japonica types – the non-glutinous varieties – share common features and tend to be plump, stubby, short-grain rice that when cooked have a somewhat sticky texture due to their moisture-retaining, starchy nature. Japonica rice types are ideal for sushi and onigiri, as these types of rice clump together when cooked and hold their shape well when pressed together. And, of course, it means it is easier to pick up and eat with chopsticks.

Glutinous rice is often cooked and pounded into a paste to create traditional *mochi* balls and dumplings.

Here are some of the most popular rice types in Asian and Japanese cooking:

White japonica 'Uruchi-mai' This 'ordinary' slightly sticky Japanese rice has had the outer layers or husk polished and removed in the milling process, which speeds its cooking time but also removes some of the nutrients, which are contained in the outer hull – however, this does make it easier to digest. It is by far the most popular rice in Japan. It is a non-glutinous rice, making it a perfect choice for those who follow a gluten-free diet. These white rice varieties are often graded by their quality, and the best quality varieties will be translucent in appearance and rounded in shape. The most highly regarded of this type of rice are hitomebore, a versatile white rice cultivated mainly in the Miyagi Prefecture and favoured for its firm texture and flavour; and koshihikari, which has a reputation as a top-quality, premium rice (*hikari* means lustrous). Slightly sweet in flavour, koshihikari 'gives' in the bite due to its tenderness when cooked. It is grown in various regions all over Japan, and has a slightly different flavour depending on which area it comes from. When cooked, the grains of japonica rice cling together, and it always needs to be thoroughly rinsed to not only clean away the outer dust but to improve the flavour.

Brown You will find most rice cookers have a different cooking setting for preparing brown rice, as the denser husk takes longer to soften; this rice hasn't been polished, and the hull and germ are intact. Most recipes suggest pre-soaking brown rice to help tenderize it prior to cooking, despite the fact that the grains of brown rice have a higher moisture content than other types. However, even when fully cooked it will remain much firmer to the bite, and it doesn't have the sticky characteristics of other japonica rice types.

Hatsuga-genmai Also known as GABA rice, this highly nutritious rice type has been allowed to germinate and begin to sprout. This happens when the rice is exposed to warm, damp atmospheres that encourage the rice grain kernels to convert some of their starches into healthy amino acids (gamma-aminobyric acid gives it the name GABA). It is also known as sprouted rice and is considered highly nutritional, as it is packed with antioxidants to help keep cholesterol levels in balance. Some people make their own GABA rice by soaking brown rice grains in room-temperature water (changing it occasionally) until the grains start

STIR-FRIED RICE

When making fried rice, Japanese people will opt for jasmine rice, also called Thai rice. These rice grains are slimmer than japonica rice varieties and release less starch when they are cooked, so they remain separate rather than clinging together. This makes it a better option for stir-frying, where the aim is to disperse the grains throughout the spices, vegetables and meats, giving the dish a 'drier', less sticky finish.

Opposite: Japonica rice formed into nagiri sushi.
Above left: Uncooked japonica rice.
Above right: Mochi balls, made with glutinous rice.

RICE FAMILIES 11

to sprout. Because the soaking process softens the grains, this type of brown or whole rice cooks more speedily than its standard brown rice counterpart.

Haiga-mai One of the more expensive rice varieties, think of this as wholemeal bread: a half-and-half brown and white variety, where the grains have been specially processed to remove the husk layer but not the germ. This makes it slightly more nutritious than pure white rice and higher in fibre too. The pale yellowish rice has a nutty flavour.

Shichibu-zuki Another wholemeal rice variety, this type is slightly closer to white rice, though it hasn't been milled to the same degree. *Buzukimai* describes the amount of milling a rice grain has undergone, and in Japanese supermarkets and rice stores it can be specified to get the exact degree of polishing you require. Along with *haiga-mai*, this rice is a good halfway house between the firmness of brown rice and the tender bite of white rice.

Musenmai This is a white rice, sometimes referred to as 'no-wash' rice. It has been 'super-cleansed', or pre-washed, to remove the residual outer coating (the *hada nuka*), meaning it doesn't require any rinsing before cooking and eating. While some people are wedded to the rinsing process to get rid of cloudiness, for those with a busy lifestyle, it cuts down on preparation time and is particularly great for breakfast rice, when time is of the essence. Purists may prefer the ritualistic rinsing preparation process, but some say *musenmai* has a better aroma and taste than washed white rice.

Mochigome In the West this type of rice is referred to more commonly as 'sticky rice'. It gets its name from its sticky texture when cooked (it is always steamed rather than boiled), which comes from the very glutinous characteristic of this variety. It is high in starch and slightly sweet to the taste, making it the rice of choice when making *mochi* (deliciously sweet rice cake balls) and other traditional sweet treats. At traditional New Year celebrations, the rice is pounded with a large wooden mallet until it becomes the rice flour used to create the sticky paste for *mochi* and *dango*, rice flour dumplings.

RICE WINE

Sake is the national drink of Japan and is a rice wine that can be brewed from any type of rice, but the preferred varieties for the most premium sake, such as *ginjo* and *daiginjo*, are specially developed rice grains known as Sakamai. The clear spirit, when made from the finest rice varieties, has fruity notes, comparable to a very dry white wine, with hints of umami, the savouriness associated with Japanese seaweed and mushrooms.

Opposite: Prepared rice flour.
Right: Polished grains of Yamada Nishiki rice.

RICE FAMILIES

Purple rice One of the oldest varieties of rice cultivated in Japan, these grains are laden with minerals and prized for their health-giving properties and used in 'medicinal' cuisine. It has a unique aroma when cooked and is considered to be stress-relieving due to its nerve-soothing minerals. It adds eye-catching colour to any dish.

Zakkoku, also known as kokumotsu gohan This is an interesting substitute for plain rice with a varied texture, as it incorporates grains, seeds, beans and even sprouts. You will often find it flecked through with black rice grains, giving it the visually appealing look of wild rice blends. It is packed with vitamins and mineral nutrients and has a high fibre content, making it good for the digestion and the slow release of energy. It is also considered to have skin benefits.

THE BENEFITS OF RICE

Rice is a versatile and satisfying ingredient, but it also has numerous nutritional benefits. As a complex carbohydrate, it releases slow-burn energy to support and restore the body's glycogen levels, to keep you going until the next meal. In fact, field workers in Japan relied on it as a crucial energy source to get them through long days working on farms.

Rice is a source of vital nutrients, including thiamine (vitamin B1), niacin (vitamin B3, which helps the body convert food into energy), vitamin E, magnesium and iron, all of which are vital for maintaining good health and preventing nutritional deficiencies.

Rice is naturally gluten-free, and it is also free from cholesterol, sugar, salt and fat. As a low-fat carboydrate, rice is a filling but heart-healthy choice, especially in a diet that emphasizes fish and vegetables.

RICE FLOUR

Rice flour is created by pounding or grinding glutinous rice or non-glutinous rice. Uruchi flour refers to the non-glutinous variety, which contains specific starches and is known as Joshinko once prepared. Rice flour retains moisture and absorbs oil at a different rate than wheat flour. While you can use rice flour in Western recipes, be aware that the result will differ from your usual wheat flour ingredient.

RICE FAMILIES

HOW TO COOK PERFECT RICE EVERY TIME

In Japan, rinsing and washing rice is an art form, with some sushi rice chefs training for two to three years just to perfect the preparation and cooking of sushi rice. But don't worry! By following these key steps, you will be able to produce delicious bowls of beautifully cooked rice every time.

WHITE RICE

This method produces enough rice for 2–3 servings.

1. Start by placing 300 grams (10.5 oz/1¼ cups) of rice in a bowl and fill it with cold water. Gently swirl the rice around with your fingers, washing it. Tip away some of the liquid, which will look cloudy, and add clean water. Repeat the process several times until the water runs clear. You can do the same thing by putting your rice in a sieve and running it under the cold tap, swirling it around, until the water runs clear.

2. Once rinsed, soak the grains in a bowl of water for around 30 minutes, before draining them thoroughly in a sieve.

3. Tip the rice into a heavy-bottomed saucepan, which will help to protect it from the heat as it cooks. Add 340 ml (11.5 fl oz) of cold water and bring the pan to the boil over a medium (not high) heat. Once boiling, put on a tight-fitting lid and turn the heat down to low. Simmer for 12 minutes, then turn off the heat.

4. Leaving the lid on, let the rice rest for a further 10 minutes to finish steaming.

5. Remove the lid and gently fluff the rice with a flat wooden spoon to release any extra steam, then serve.

BROWN RICE

This method produces enough for 2–3 servings.

1. In a bowl, run 300 g (10.5 oz/1¼ cups) of brown rice under the cold tap, swirling the grains with your fingertips to move it around and clean every grain. Drain away cloudy water as you go, continuing until the water runs clear.

2. Tip the rice into a heavy-bottomed saucepan, which will help to protect the rice

from the heat as it cooks. Add water at a ratio of two parts rice to three parts water. Place a fitted lid on the pan and bring it to the boil over a medium heat.

3. When it is boiling, turn the heat down to low and allow the rice to simmer for 15–20 minutes, until the rice has absorbed all the liquid. Don't be tempted to lift the lid during this time.

4. Turn off the heat and allow the rice to sit for 10 minutes to finish steaming and to soften. You can leave it to sit for longer for an even softer texture.

5. Once steamed, fluff the rice up with a flat wooden spoon and serve.

GLUTINOUS RICE

There are various ways to cook glutinous rice, and different Asian countries have their preferred methods. Here is my foolproof method when using short-grained, mochigome glutinous rice.

You will need a large, lidded saucepan, a steaming basket (preferably bamboo, but metal works fine too), or a steamer balanced on a tin.

When handling sticky rice, wet your utensils and your hands, as it will help the rice grains from sticking to them. It is also a good idea to line your steamer dish with parchment paper to prevent the rice from sticking to it. Glutinous rice dries out fast, so cover it with a damp cloth until you are ready to serve.

For two people, weigh 300 g (10.5 oz/1¼ cups) of glutinous rice.

1. Rinse the glutinous rice in a sieve under the cold tap quickly (you can get away with not rinsing this rice at all if you prefer, or if you are in a rush). Put it in a bowl and fill with water, making sure the water generously covers the rice (which will expand) and pre-soak the rice

STORE CUPBOARD RICE SEASONING

Add flavour to a plain bowl of Japanese rice with a sprinkle of *furikake*. This savoury-sweet condiment is a blend of sesame seeds, nori seaweed, dried fish flakes or chili flakes, miso powder, salt and sugar, which provides a deliciously authentic umami taste.

for 24–48 hours before cooking.

2. After soaking, drain off any remaining water and spread the rice out on the parchment-lined steamer dish. Remember not to layer more than 5–8 cm (2–3 inches) of rice, as it all needs to cook evenly. If making a larger quantity, you may want to cook it in batches.

3. Add water to a large saucepan, making sure it is below where the steamer will sit. Place the steamer dish into the pan, balancing it on a rack or tin if needed, and place a lid on the pot.

4. Bring the water to a gentle boil, then simmer on a low heat for 30–45 minutes. After 30 minutes, check the consistency and steam longer as required.

RICE COOKER METHOD

Because the Japanese eat rice with nearly every meal, preparing it using a rice cooker is one of the simplest ways to enjoy this staple. They don't take up much room and, once you work out the basics, are easy to use and very dependable, making them a worthwhile investment.

Timing is easy too; your rice cooker will have a different time setting for brown rice, so make sure you follow the instructions according to the amount and type you are making.

The key is getting the correct rice to water ratio. Rice cookers have a measuring cup included, making it easy to pour out the correct ratios, with clear water-fill line markings for white or brown rice water.

Most rice cookers have a sweet or sticky rice mode, as glutinous rice absorbs water quickly so needs a slightly shorter cooking time than white short grain rice.

KEEPING AND STORING RICE

If you have leftovers of rice dishes or simply make too much, there are some guidelines you need to stick to in order to enjoy eating it again. Storing rice at room temperature is risky due to the potential for food poisoning, so follow these guidelines for safer rice storage.

Spread any leftover warm rice on a flat tray to let it cool as quickly as possible and remove any steam. Leave it to cool no longer than 2 hours.

Once cooled, put it in a covered container and chill it in the fridge.

Although some food safety organisations suggest longer, I keep leftover rice for no more than 48 hours in the fridge before reheating it.

You can reheat your rice however you choose, but when reheating make sure that all the grains are piping hot all the way through. Check this by forking through the grains halfway through reheating.

You can also store cooked rice in the freezer, but again make sure it is thoroughly defrosted in the fridge and reheated throughout before consuming.

Don't cool, reheat, then cool again. Rice that is still leftover from a first reheating needs to be thrown away.

Don't be tempted to eat rice that has been left out for longer than 2 hours. A takeaway box may look tempting the next morning but should be avoided.

KNOW YOUR NOODLES

For noodle heads, knowing the difference between the different types of rice noodles can make the difference between a good dish and an exceptional dish. Broadly speaking, there are two main players in the noodle game.

Vermicelli

Vermicelli noodles are ultra-skinny threads of long noodles, most commonly used in Southeast Asian recipes. Usually made from rice flour or wheat flour, they can also be formed from semolina (not to be confused with noodles made from mung bean flour, which are known as cellophane or glass noodles). Because of their slender nature, vermicelli work well in these dishes:

• Soup bowls, to add bulk without overwhelming the liquid base.
• Stir-fries, as they can be worked into the ingredients with ease.
• Cold Asian noodle salads, as their slightly chewy texture means they pair well with crunchy salad vegetables.
• Sweet desserts, as they can be wound into nests.

Rice noodles

Rice noodles are gluten-free noodles made in a variety of shapes and sizes, such as flat, thin versions that resemble tagliatelle and thicker, spaghetti-like shapes. They are made from rice flour and water and are a staple in many Asian dishes. They especially suited to these dishes:

• Stir fries: as with vermicelli, rice noodles combine well with stir-fry ingredients.
• Pad Thai: flat, wide noodles give this dish its unique appearance and edibility.
• Pho: a Vietnamese soup dish, akin to ramen, which is a large, satisfying meal in a bowl.
• Spring rolls: round, rolled noodles create a satisfying filling when paired with a vegetable or meat filling.

HANDY STORE CUPBOARD BASICS

There are a few things that are great to have as store cupboard basics, allowing you to create myriad Japanese and Asian dishes. Most of them are fermented or dried so have a long shelf life.

• Mirin (Japanese sweet rice wine)
• Japanese soy sauce (a thinner version of traditional soy sauce)
• Cooking sake
• Fish sauce
• Gochujang (Korean chili paste)
• Japanese pepper (dried spice)
• Dried bonito flakes (fish flakes)
• Dried kelp stock (powdered flavouring)
• Wasabi powder
• Miso powder, or miso paste in a tube
• Tamarind paste (for dumpling dipping sauces)
• Tenmenjiang (sweet bean sauce)

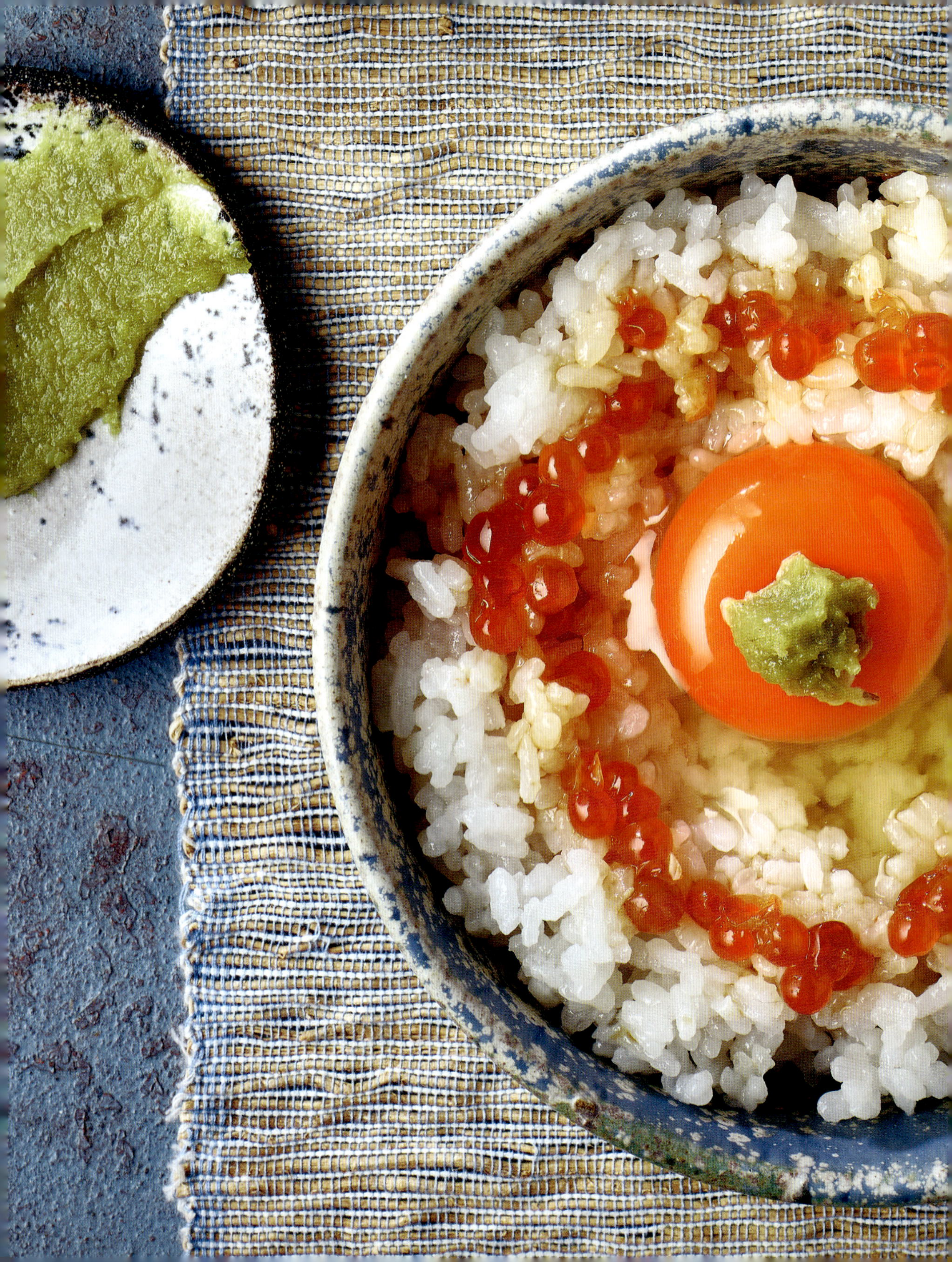

KAKE GOHAN

You may not have discovered *kake gohan* in your local café or diner, but this delicious rice-based bowl is a traditional Japanese breakfast dish. It often features fresh raw eggs that thicken slightly on contact with the warm rice, adding a creamy and satisfying texture to the bowl. Not only is it a great comfort food, but with tasty additions, it makes a nutritious breakfast alternative to sweet pastries and cereals. Spiced up with a little chilli or flecked with fresh green vegetables, along with the egg it is the ultimate protein bowl, guaranteed to keep you going until lunchtime. Given its creamy texture, it also makes a perfect standby supper dish substitute for risotto.

TAMAKAKE GOHAN

Serves 1

If you are just starting your *kake gohan* journey, this simple dish will make a great introductory recipe. As you become familiar with the dish, you can build in extra toppings and garnishes of your choice.

---

200 grams (7 oz/1 cup) warm japonica rice
1 medium (US large) organic egg
1 spring onion (scallion), finely chopped
1 pinch sea salt
1 teaspoon sesame oil

1. After cooking the rice (see page 14), tip it into a small bowl where it can remain warm. Make a well in the middle of the rice and crack in the whole raw egg. Sprinkle the chopped spring onion around the edges of the egg and dust sea salt over the top of the rice.

2. Spoon a teaspoon of sesame oil on top of the egg, then using chopsticks, mix everything together well. In just a few moments, the heat from the rice will lightly cook the egg, making it ready to enjoy.

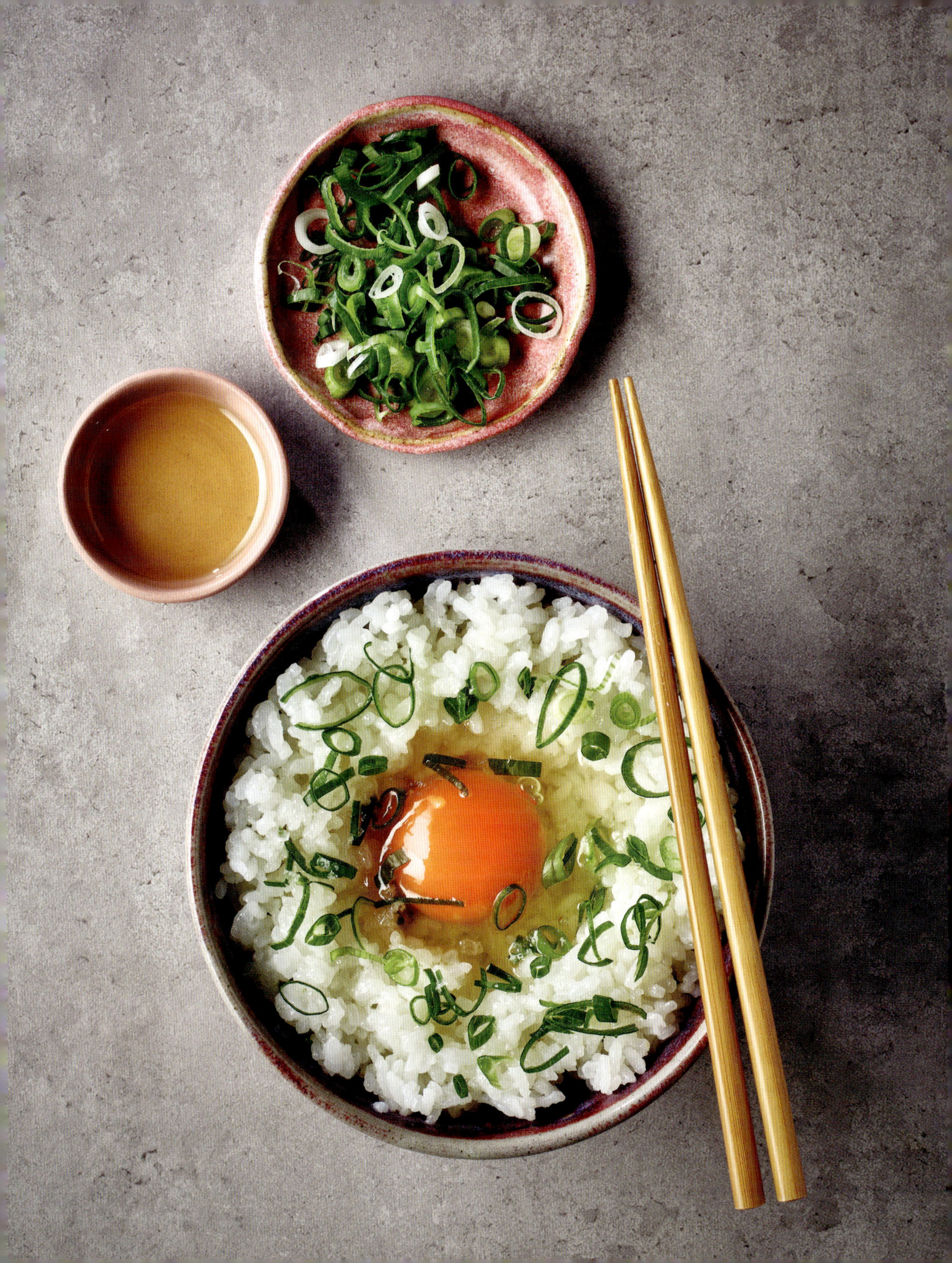

KIMCHI TAMAGO GOHAN

Serves 1

The plain and simple nature of *kake gohan* pairs beautifully with the bright, tangy, sour notes of kimchi. This recipe also offers a great way to get your daily fermented food quota.

---

200 grams (7 oz/1 cup) warm japonica rice
1 medium (US large) organic egg
1 tablespoon kimchi
1 teaspoon Japanese soy sauce
2 sheets Korean seaweed (or seasoned nori)

1. After cooking the rice (see page 14), tip it into a small bowl where it can remain warm. Make a well in the middle and crack in the whole raw egg. Now spoon in the kimchi, nestling it beside the raw egg and sprinkle Korean seaweed – breaking it up with your fingertips – over the top of the egg. Enjoy.

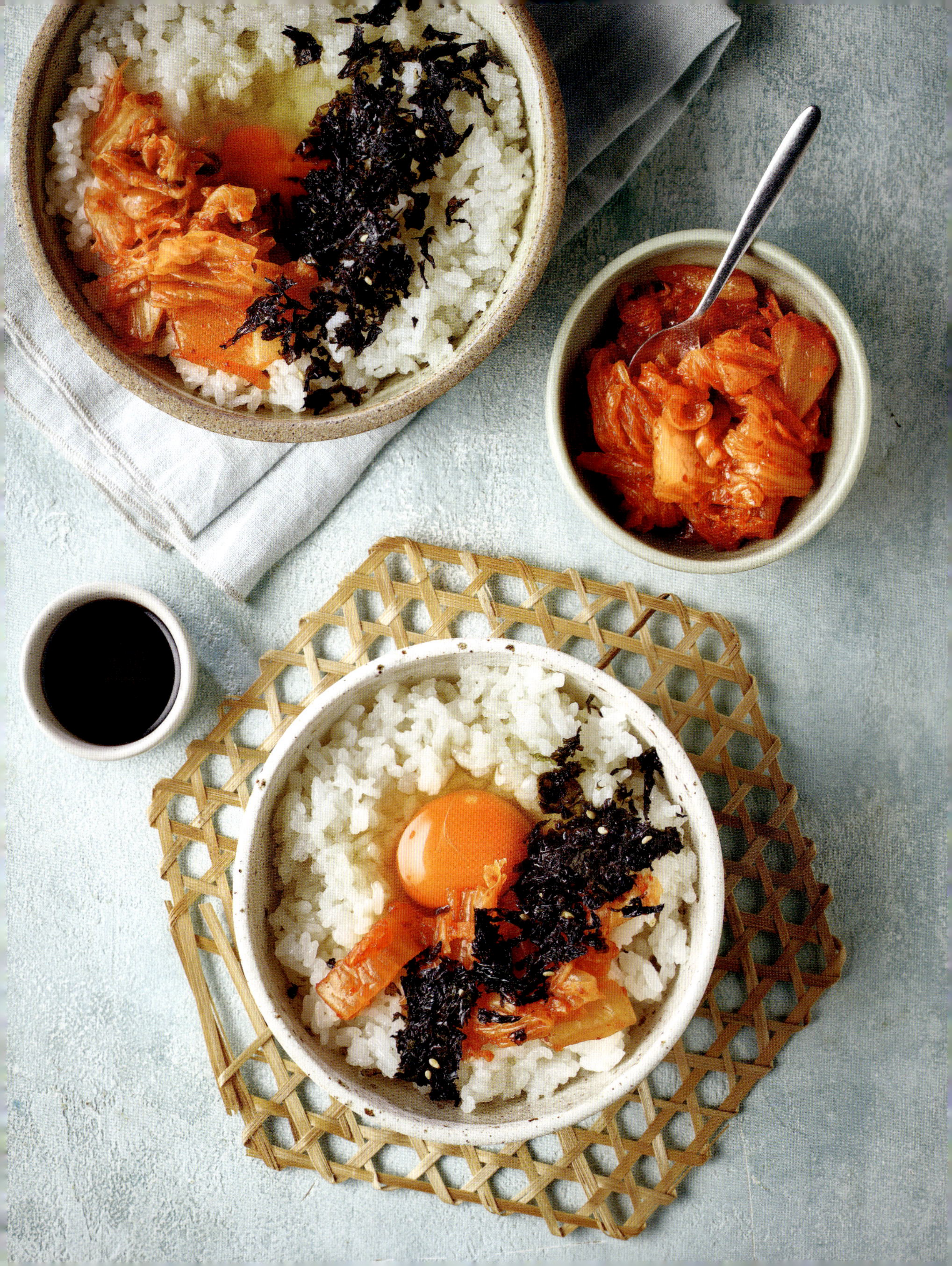

DOUBLE EGGS GOHAN

Serves 1

This dish requires its flavouring elements to be chilled for a couple of hours. However, it takes only moments to prepare and you can have all of your flavourings ready-to-go in advance. The recipe calls for salmon roe (known as *ikura* in Japan), which you can buy at most good supermarkets; it will add a little delicious extravagance to your morning meal.

200 grams (7 oz/1 cup) warm japonica rice
1 medium (US large) organic egg
30 grams (1 oz/2 tablespoons) *ikura* (salmon roe)
Pea-sized squeeze of wasabi paste (optional)

Marinade
3 tablespoons Japanese soy sauce
1 tablespoon mirin
1 tablespoon cooking sake
1 tablespoon water

See the chapter opener for this recipe's image.

1. Put the soy sauce, mirin, sake and water into a small saucepan over a medium heat. Bring it to a boil and allow to bubble for 2 minutes, then remove the pan from the heat and set it aside to cool.

2. Once the sauce is cool, pour it into a small lidded container and add the *ikura*. Put the lid on and refrigerate for 2 hours.

3. At the end of the marinating time, cook the rice (see page 14) and tip it into a small bowl where it can remain warm. Make a well in the middle and crack in the raw egg.

4. Spoon the marinated *ikura* mixture around the raw egg, then squeeze the wasabi over the centre of the egg yolk, to add an enlivening hit of fresh heat.

EGGY BUTTER RICE

Serves 2

This recipe has its roots in a Chinese version known as lard soy sauce rice. Various interpretations of the dish have sprung up, because it is so easy to make and delightfully satisfying. Rich with egg and butter, it delivers the tang of Worcestershire sauce and the fragrance of roasted garlic.

---

300 grams (10½ oz/1½ cups) warm rice
Generous knob (pat) of unsalted butter
3 medium (US large) eggs
1 teaspoon roasted garlic powder
Splash of Worcestershire sauce
Salt and pepper, to taste

1. After cooking the rice (see page 14), set it aside in its pan. Heat a frying pan over a low heat and add the butter. While the butter melts, beat the eggs in a small bowl.

2. Tip the eggs into the pan and cook over a low heat, stirring them lightly so they fluff a little. While they are still soft and creamy, add the cooked rice to the pan and turn up the heat to medium. Stir-fry until the rice and eggs are mixed in together, but avoid overcooking the eggs (this can make them rubbery).

3. Quickly add in the roasted garlic powder and the Worcestershire sauce and mix. Season with salt and pepper to taste, and adjust if necessary. It's ready!

PROTEIN BOWL TAMORI DON

Serves 1

This take on *kake gohan* is laden with protein, packing an energy punch first thing in the morning. The warmth of ginger and chilli make it a great option for cooler autumnal days when you want your immune system to be at its best. *Oba* leaf, or *shiso*, adds fresh, herby, mild and minty flavours.

---

200 grams (7 oz/1 cup) warm japonica rice
150 grams (5 oz) silken tofu
1 medium (US large) poached egg
1 spring onion (scallion), stalk only, sliced
3 shredded green shiso (perilla) leaves
1 tablespoon chilli oil
1 tablespoon Japanese soy sauce
Freshly grated myoga (Japanese ginger) or fresh root ginger/pickled ginger, to taste

1. After cooking the rice (see page 14), tip it into a small bowl where it can remain warm. Put a pan of water on to boil, for the poached egg. In the meantime, crumble the tofu into your desired size. Top the rice with the crumbled tofu, and sprinkle the spring onion and shiso leaves over the top.

2. Now poach your egg in a small saucepan. When it is ready, make a small well in the middle of the tofu and rice, then nestle the poached egg into it.

3. Drizzle with the chilli oil and soy sauce and top with grated *myoga*.

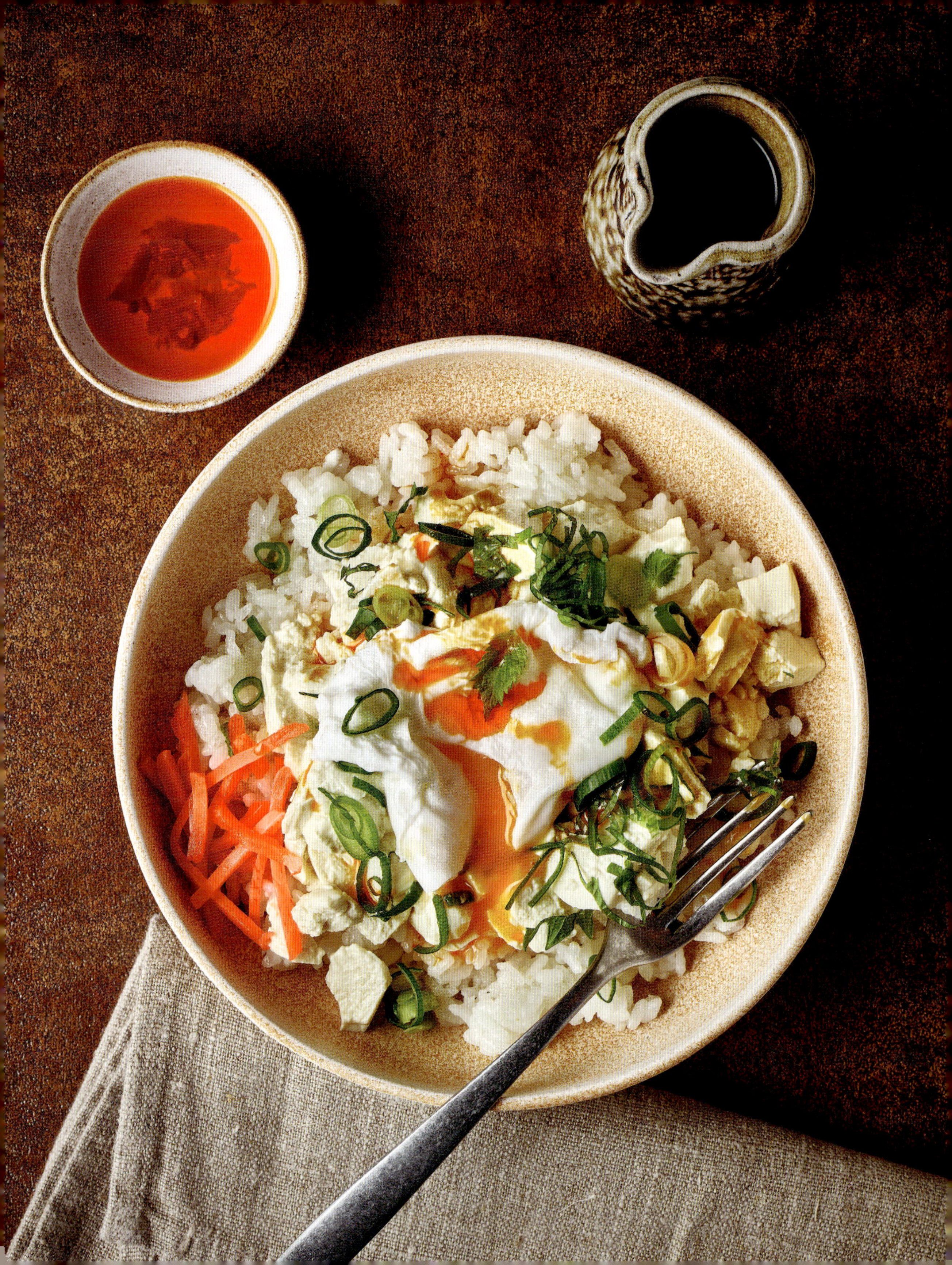

WASABI-FLAVOURED AVOCADO & EGG RICE

Serves 1

Instead of your usual caffeine hit in the morning, why not sample this Japanese breakfast dish with its enlivening hit of wasabi. The heat of the jade-green paste will revive your senses in moments. Coupled with the refreshing avocado and protein-rich salty tuna, it makes a great start to the day.

---

200 grams (7 oz/1 cup) warm japonica rice
½ avocado
1 tablespoon Japanese soy sauce
½ teaspoon wasabi paste
35 grams (1 oz) canned tuna (in oil)
1 sheet dried nori seaweed
1 medium (US large) organic egg

1. After cooking the rice (see page 14), tip it into a small bowl where it can remain warm.

2. In the meantime, while the rice is cooking, halve the avocado and remove the stone (pit). Peel and cut the flesh into 1-cm (½-inch) cubes.

3. Mix the soy sauce and wasabi in a bowl. Flake the tuna with a fork, then add to the soy sauce mix along with the avocado cubes and mix gently. Leave to marinate for about 10 minutes.

4. Top the rice bowl with the marinated avocado and tuna mixture. Make a well in the middle of the bowl and crack the raw egg into it.

5. Chop or break the nori seaweed into small pieces, and sprinkle it over the top to finish.

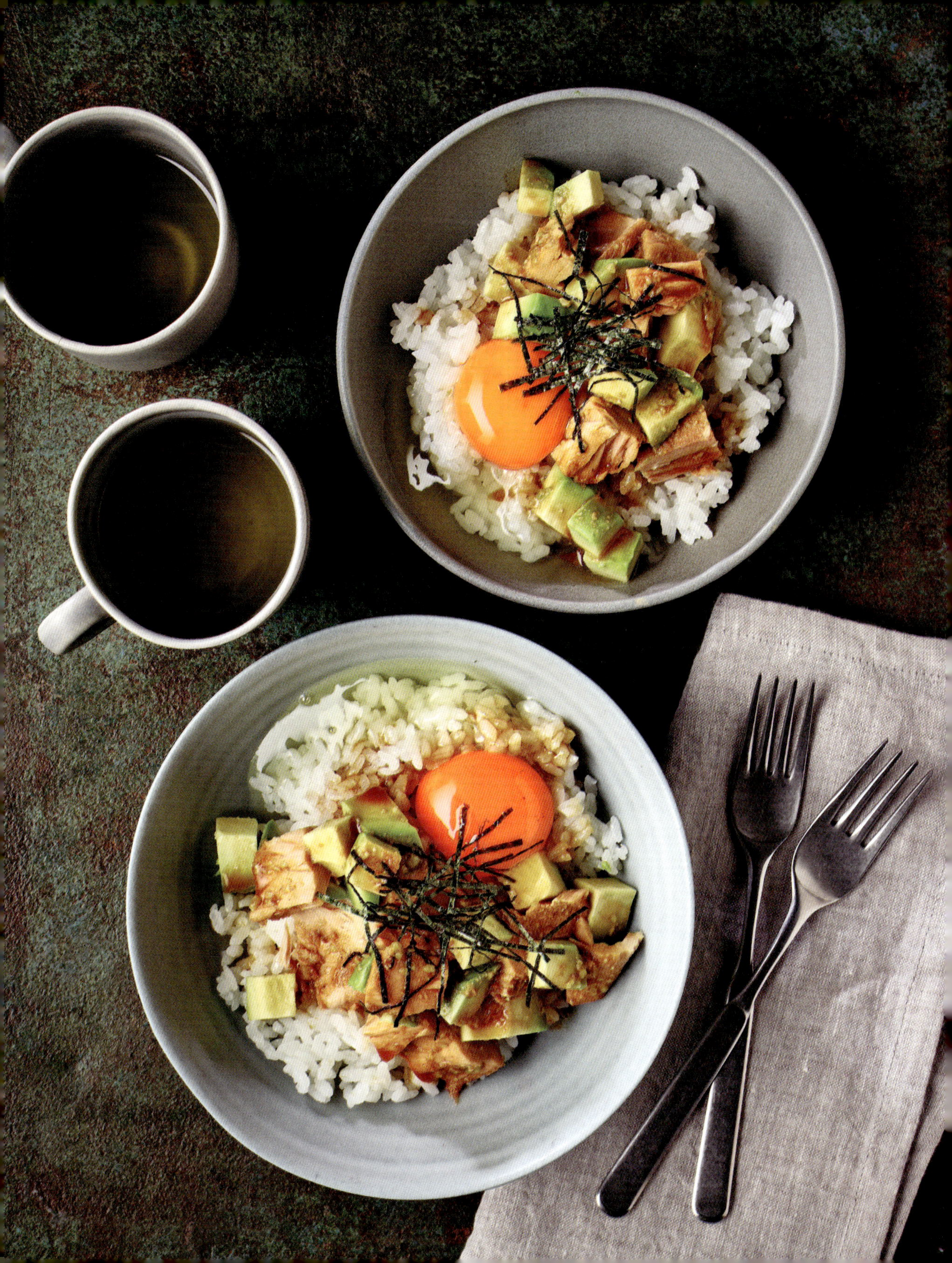

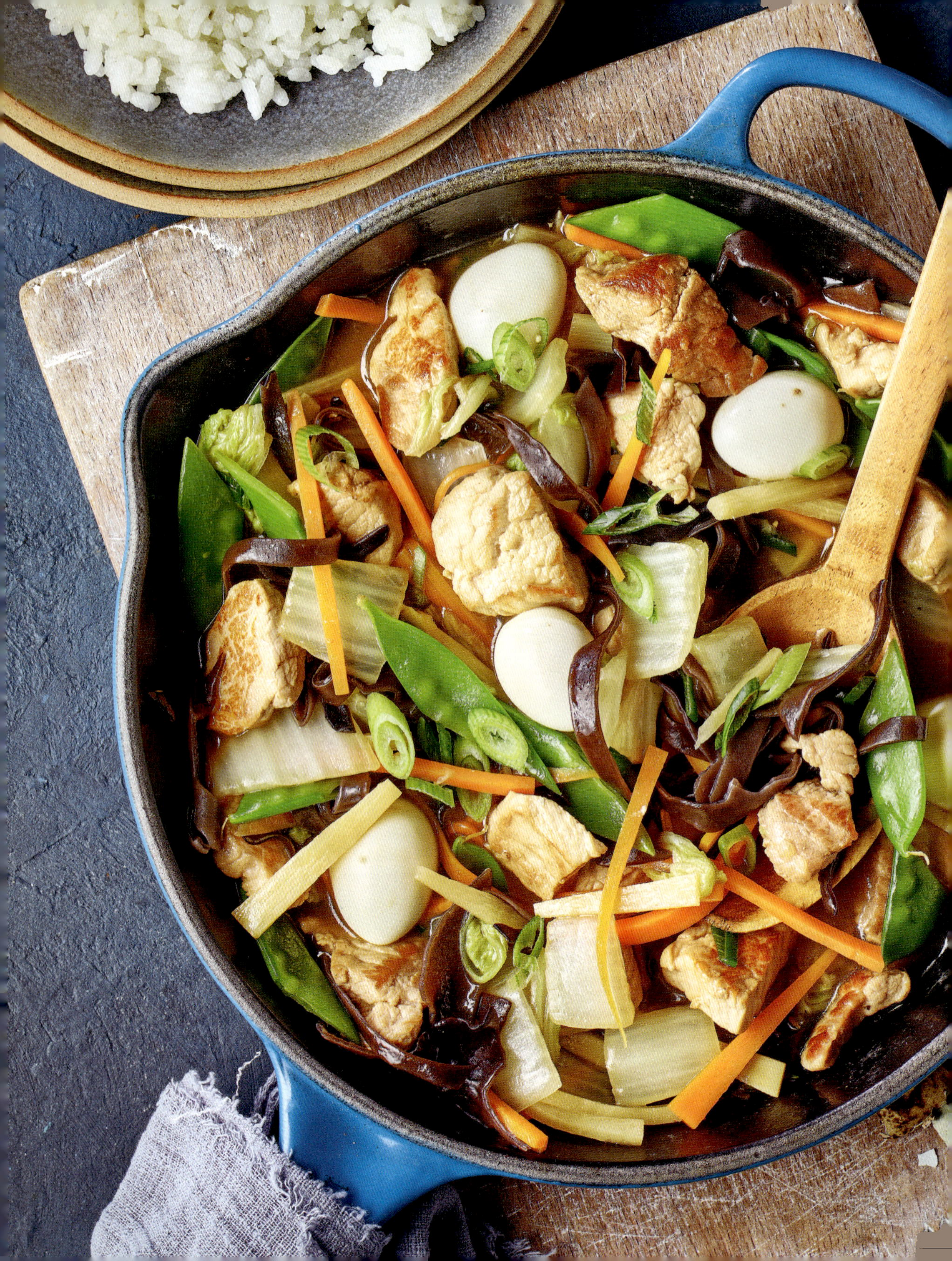

DONBURI

A Japanese *donburi* is a "rice bowl" with a main dish served over the top. In Japan it is simply referred to as *don*. It is a warm, comforting and satisfying dish, with the option for many different sauce-simmered meats, fish and vegetables to be served with it. To really indulge in *don*, seek out oversized dishes so you have room to ladle your toppings over the bed of rice.

GYUDON

Serves 2

This *gyudon*, or beef bowl, is easy to make and takes much less time than a British beef stew. The super tasty sauce in this dish has an array of Asian flavours enhanced with softened, soaked onions. To sample this dish in the most authentic way, try adding a soft-boiled egg on top, turning it into a *gyu-toji-don*.

---

300 grams (10½ oz/1½ cups) japonica rice
200 grams (7 oz) rump (sirloin) beef strips
Pickled ginger, to taste

Sauce
½ white onion, sliced into 8 wedges
1 tablespoon cooking sake
2 tablespoons mirin
2 teaspoons sugar
2 tablespoons Japanese soy sauce
½ teaspoon freshly grated root ginger
200 ml (7 fl oz/scant 1 cup) water

1. Cook the japonica rice according to the packet instructions (it will be ready in roughly the same time you prepare the beef in the sauce).

2. Meanwhile, slice the onion into wedges and put them into a saucepan over high heat with the sake, mirin, sugar, soy sauce, grated ginger and water, and bring to the boil. Once boiling, turn the heat down to medium, cover and simmer for 5 minutes.

3. Meanwhile, if the beef strips are on the large side, slice them to make thin strips (this will ensure quick cooking and tender beef). Add the thin beef strips to the sauce and simmer over a low heat for 10 minutes, skimming off any residue that rises to the surface.

4. Place the warm, cooked rice in two bowls and scoop over the beef and sauce.

5. Top with the fragrant, pickled ginger.

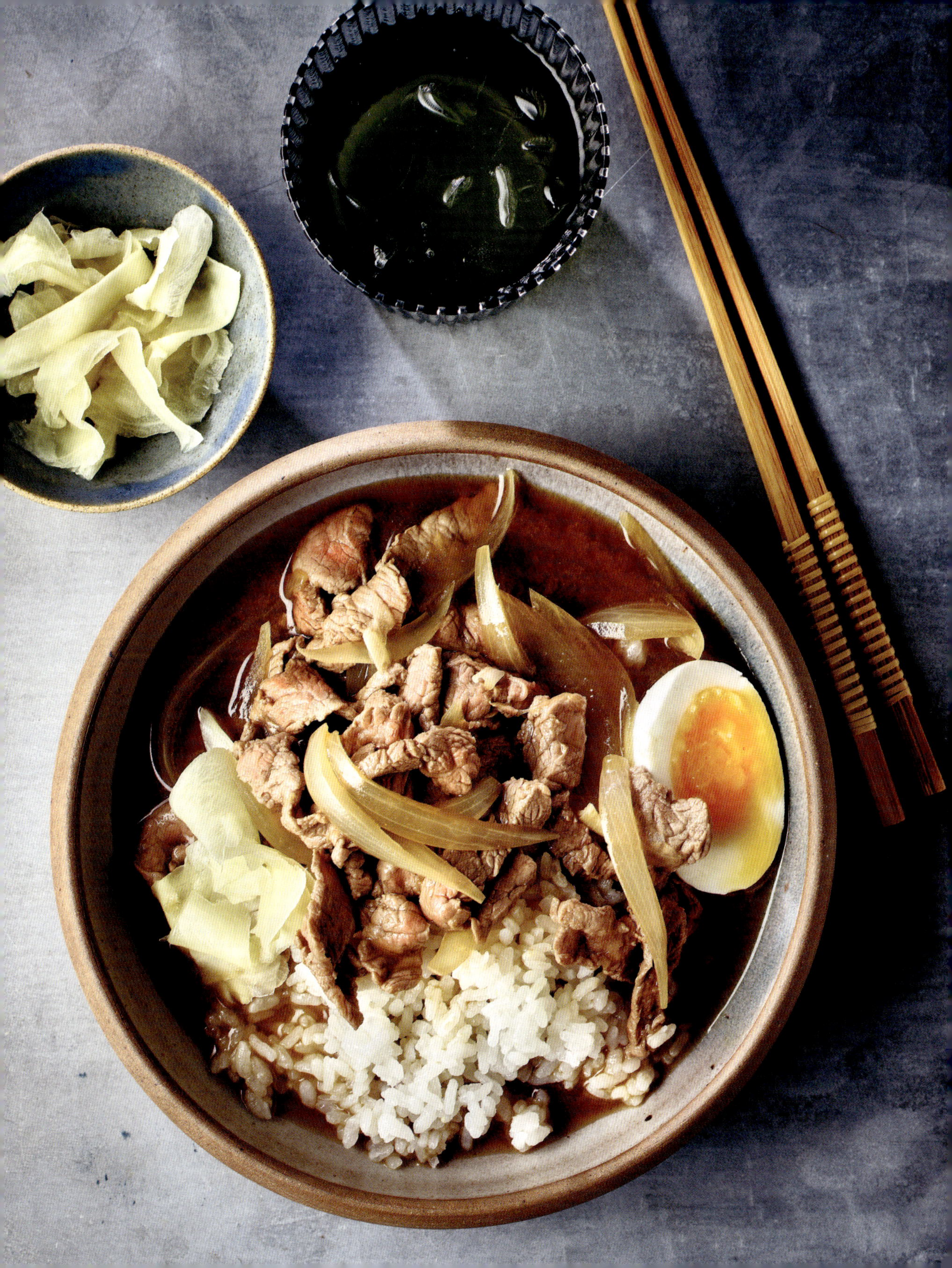

KATSU DON

Serves 1

Katsu don is a classic and filling dish. The crispy fried *katsu* adds crunch and texture to the dish that slowly melts into the broth. With a little practice, this is a dish that will become a go-to and is guaranteed to replace a Friday night takeout. Whole pork loin is often an overlooked ingredient, but not only is it an affordable meat, it requires very little cooking time to deliver soft, tender and lean deliciousness. Protein is a vital part of any diet, and this dish provides a protein-rich boost with a truly tasty sauce.

---

150 grams (5 oz/¾ cup) japonica rice
120 grams (4 oz) pork loin
Vegetable oil
2 medium (US large) eggs
25 grams chives, cut into 2-cm (¾-inch) pieces

Breadcrumbs
1 medium (US large) egg
Plain (all-purpose) flour
Handful of breadcrumbs
Salt and pepper

Sauce
¼ white onion, sliced
50 ml (1½ fl oz/scant ¼ cup) water
1 tablespoon Japanese soy sauce
1 tablespoon mirin
1 tablespoon cooking sake
1½ teaspoons sugar
1 teaspoon chicken stock powder

1. Remove any sinew or tendons from the pork loin. Place the loin on a flat board and cover the top with a sheet of cling film (plastic wrap). Pound the covered loin with a rolling pin to flatten and tenderize it. Remove the cling film and sprinkle a pinch of salt and pepper on both sides.

2. Now beat one of the eggs in a shallow dish. Coat the seasoned loin by covering it in the flour, followed by the beaten egg and then the breadcrumbs.

3. Meanwhile, cook the japonica rice according to the packet instructions.

4. Heat the oil in a small frying pan to 170°C (340°F). Place the breaded pork in the pan and fry for 5–7 minutes, turning the pork occasionally, until the inside of the meat is cooked through and the surface has browned. Set aside.

5. When cool enough to handle, cut the breaded pork into 2-cm (¾-inch) widths.

6. For the sauce, put the sliced onion, water, soy sauce, mirin, sake, sugar and chicken stock powder into a saucepan and simmer over a medium heat for 2–3 minutes.

7. When the onion has softened, place the pork on top of the sauce and top with the remainder of the lightly beaten egg, keeping the heat at medium. Cover, turn off the heat, and steam for 30 seconds.

8. Put your cooked rice into a bowl and slide the sauce and pork topped with steamed egg over the rice. Sprinkle with chives and it's ready to eat!

OYAKODON

Serves 1

Oyakodon is a very famous and popular dish in Japan. The reason it is so beloved comes down to its name. *Oya* means "parent" in Japanese, while *ko* is "child" – and this dish is all about the chicken and the egg. The eggs are added in two batches to create extra texture and richness. Make it whenever you are looking for a heartier alternative to chicken soup.

---

150 grams (5 oz/¾ cup) japonica rice
¼ white onion
120 grams (4 oz) boneless chicken thigh
2 medium (US large) eggs, beaten
1 spring onion (scallion), sliced diagonally, to garnish
Togarashi, shichimi or chilli sauce, to serve (optional)

Sauce
1 tablespoon cooking sake
1 tablespoon mirin
1 teaspoon sugar
1 tablespoon Japanese soy sauce
3 tablespoons water

1. Prepare your japonica rice according to the packet instructions (it will be ready in roughly the same time as it takes to prepare the topping).
2. Now slice the onion thinly. Trim any excess fat from the chicken thigh meat and cut it into bite-sized pieces.
3. For the sauce, heat the sake, mirin, sugar, soy sauce and water in a frying pan over a medium heat, stirring to mix everything well. Once simmering, add the sliced onion and chicken pieces. Bring it back to a simmer, then cover with a lid and simmer over a low-medium heat for around 5 minutes, until the meat is cooked through and the onion is soft.
4. Remove the lid, turn up the heat to medium and simmer, until the liquid has reduced. Pour in two thirds of the beaten eggs, cover and cook over medium heat for around 1 minute.
5. Now pour in the remaining egg mixture, cover and cook for about 10 seconds.
6. Place your cooked rice in a serving bowl, top with the creamy chicken and egg dish and dot with vibrant spring onions.

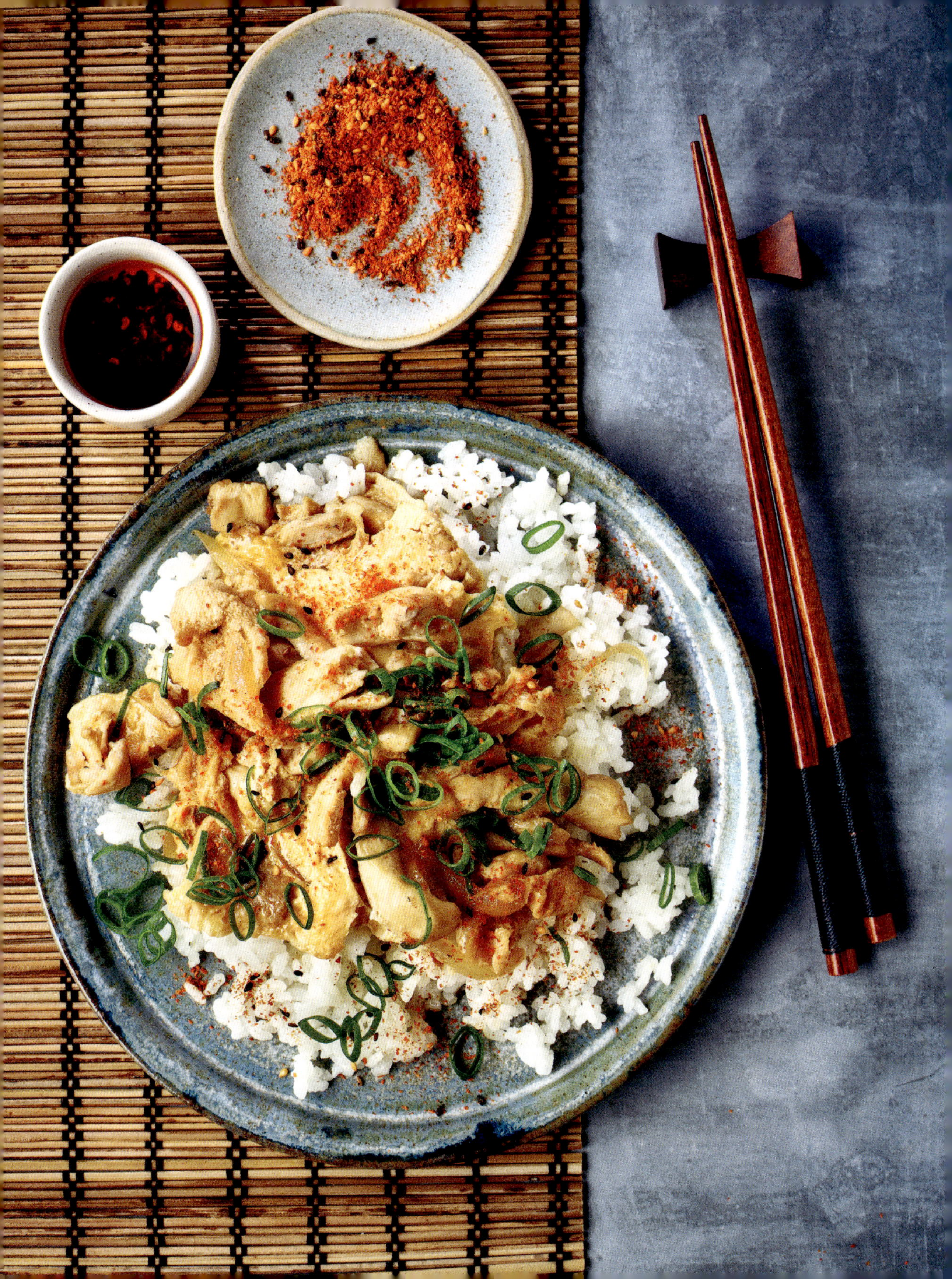

CHUUKADON

Serves 2

Chuukadon showcases vegetables and for those looking for a vegetarian option with a difference, this is bursting with unique Asian veggies. The key here is to cook the vegetables over a high heat, and fast, to retain their texture and add crunch to the dish.

---

100 grams (3½ oz) pork loin, diced
160 grams (5½ oz) Chinese (napa) cabbage
50 grams (2 oz) tinned, sliced bamboo shoots
25 grams (1 oz) carrot
50g (2 oz) dried wood ear mushrooms
1 spring onion (scallion), green stalk only
6 mangetout (snow peas)
300 grams (10½ oz/1½ cups) japonica rice
1 tablespoon sesame oil
1 tablespoon cooking sake
scant ½ teaspoon sugar
scant ½ teaspoon salt
1 tablespoon Japanese soy sauce
scant ½ teaspoon chicken stock powder
200 ml (7 fl oz/scant 1 cup) water
6 quail's eggs, soft-boiled and peeled
1 tablespoon cornflour (cornstarch), dissolved in 1 tablespoon of water
Salt and pepper

1. First, season the pork with salt and pepper.
2. Separate the Chinese cabbage into stalks and leaves, and cut them all into bite-sized pieces.. Cut the carrots into 3-mm (¼-inch) thin strips.
3. Soak the wood ear mushrooms in water for 15 minutes, drain, cut off the stalks and slice into strips. Meanwhile, thinly slice the spring onion diagonally. Remove the strings from the mangetout and cut them in half diagonally.
4. Prepare your japonica rice according to the packet instructions (it will be ready in roughly the same time as it takes to prepare the topping dish).
5. Meanwhile, heat the sesame oil in a frying pan over a medium heat, add the chopped pork and stir-fry until the meat changes colour. Add the Chinese cabbage stalks, bamboo shoots and carrots and stir-fry until soft.
6. Add the Chinese cabbage leaves, wood ear mushrooms and spring onion and stir-fry briefly until the oil is evenly distributed.

7. Add the sake, sugar, salt, soy sauce, chicken stock powder and water to the mixture. Stir the mixture to combine, add the quail eggs, then bring to a boil over a high heat. Once it comes to the boil, add the mangetout and stir, then pour in the dissolved cornflour and heat, while stirring, until it thickens.

8. Place the cooked rice in two bowls and spoon the topping over.

TOFU DON

Serves 2

Zen Buddhism is an ancient religion in Japan, and as part of the monks' training they must abstain from eating meat or fish. Instead, they follow a diet known as *shojin* cuisine. This way of eating led to alternative protein options, such as tofu, becoming greatly appreciated; this versatile, meat-free ingredient is a common feature in both the monks' culinary culture and throughout Japan.

---

150 grams/5 oz firm tofu
1 tablespoon cornflour (cornstarch)
300 grams (10½ oz/1½ cups) japonica rice
1 tablespoon olive oil
Handful of spinach, rinsed thoroughly
100 ml (3½ fl oz/scant ½ cup) water
1 tablespoon cooking sake
1 tablespoon mirin
½ teaspoon sugar
1½ tablespoons Japanese soy sauce
½ teaspoon dry kelp powder
2 medium (US large) eggs, well beaten

1. Wrap the tofu in kitchen paper towels and place on a heat-resistant plate, then microwave at 600W for 2 minutes. Drain away any excess liquid and dispose of the kitchen paper. Allow to cool, then cut the block of tofu into 2-cm (¾-inch) cubes and dust all over with cornflour.

2. In the meantime, prepare your japonica rice according to the packet instructions (it will be ready in roughly the same time as it takes to prepare the topping dish).

3. Heat the olive oil in a frying pan, add in the tofu cubes and fry over a medium heat, turning them around until all the surfaces have browned.

4. Add the spinach leaves, water, sake, mirin, sugar, soy sauce and dry kelp powder. Gently mix these together and bring the mixture to a boil. Once boiling, cover the frying pan with a lid, lower the heat and simmer for 2 minutes.

5. Remove the lid and add in the well-beaten eggs, stirring frequently. Cover again and cook over low-medium heat for about 1 minute until the eggs are half-cooked.

6. Place the rice in two bowls and pour over the tasty tofu mixture.

TENDON

Serves 2

For those craving the air-light crunch of tempura, this dish delivers. The crispy batter and sweet and spicy tempura sauce are a perfect combination. The word *tendon*, a shortened version of *tempura-don*, is the local way of asking for this bowl. Tempura is a technique that arrived in Japan in the 16th century with the Portuguese missionaries, who coated food with flour and water for frying. It is now a signature of authentic Japanese cookery. For great tempura, don't over-work the batter or it will become too dense – and always use chilled water to ensure it is extra crispy.

---

300 grams (10½ oz/1½ cups) japonica rice
4 headless prawns (shrimp)
½ aubergine (eggplant)
4 asparagus spears
2 whole shiitake mushrooms
Vegetable oil

Tempura batter
1 medium (US large) egg
150 ml (5 fl oz/⅔ cup) ice-cold water (kept refrigerated until using)
100 grams (3½ oz/scant 1 cup) tempura flour, plus a little extra for coating

Sauce
2 tablespoons mirin
1 tablespoon sugar
2 tablespoons Japanese soy sauce
scant ½ teaspoon chicken stock powder
100 ml (3 fl oz/scant ½ cup) water

1. Start by preparing your batter. Crack the egg into a bowl and mix, then add the chilled water and mix again. Add the flour and mix quickly with chopsticks, leaving a few lumps. (If you mix too much, the batter will not be crispy). Once mixed, return it to the fridge until ready to use.

2. Peel the prawns, leaving the tails on, and use a sharp knife to remove the vein down the back. Make 3-4 cuts on the underside with a knife. Coat the prawns lightly with tempura flour.

3. Cut the stalk off the aubergine, and slice it into thin pieces. Trim the bottom half of the asparagus and cut each one into thirds. Remove the stalks from the shiitake mushrooms and make a cross-cut under each mushroom cap.

4. In the meantime, prepare your japonica rice according to the packet instructions (it will be ready in roughly the same time as it takes to prepare the topping dish).

5. Now make the sauce by putting the mirin, sugar, soy sauce, chicken stock powder and water into a saucepan over a high heat. Bring it to a simmer, then cook on a low heat for about 2 minutes until reduced by two thirds. Set aside.

6. Finally, deep-fry the tempura: fill a separate deep saucepan about half-full with the oil and heat to 170°C (340°F). Coat the aubergine, asparagus and shiitake mushrooms in the batter and fry for 1–2 minutes. When they float to the surface (indicating they are done), remove with a skimmer and drain on kitchen paper towels. Next, coat the prawns in batter and fry for 1–2 minutes until they float to the surface, then remove and drain.

7. Dive your cooked rice between two serving bowls, top with a selection of tempura and pour the sauce over it all.

BIBIMBAP DON

Serves 2

Koreans have made bowls of *bibimbap don* for centuries. It is thought that in rural areas, the wives of farmers, who had little time to spare, started making it as a time-saving option. It became the perfect recipe for taking leftover vegetables, meat or whatever was to hand and adding rice, thereby creating an inexpensive, no-waste meal-in-a-bowl.

300 grams (10½ oz/1½ cups) japonica rice
1 tablespoon sesame oil
150 grams (5 oz) minced (ground) beef
½ teaspoon grated ginger
½ teaspoon grated garlic
1 tablespoon cooking sake
1 teaspoon sugar
1½ teaspoons gochujang (Korean red chilli paste)
1 tablespoon Japanese soy sauce
½ pack beansprouts
25 grams (1 oz) carrot
150 grams (5¼ oz) or 5-cm (2-inch) piece daikon (mooli)
Handful of spinach leaves, thoroughly rinsed
¼ teaspoon salt
2 medium (US large) eggs, soft-boiled or poached
2 sheets Korean seaweed

1. Prepare your japonica rice according to the packet instructions (it will be ready in roughly the same time as it takes to prepare the topping dish).

2. Heat the sesame oil in a frying pan over a low-medium heat and add in the minced meat and grated ginger and garlic. Break the meat up with a wooden spatula as you stir-fry until it changes colour. To the same pan, add the sake, sugar, *gochujang* and soy sauce and stir-fry for around 1 more minute to infuse the beef in the spicy, sweet flavours.

3. Slice the roots off the beansprouts and halve them lengthways. Add them to a small pan of water and boil for 2 minutes. Remove with a slotted spoon. Shred the carrots and add them to the same pan and boil for 1 minute. Remove them, then slice the daikon and boil it for 1 minute. Now add the spinach to the same water and boil for 1 minute.

4. In a small saucepan boil some water and the eggs until soft-boiled (or poach them if you prefer).

5. Once ready, divide your prepared rice between two serving bowls and place half of the sweet, spicy minced meat on top. Place each vegetable individually on top of the rice around the spicy meat, then add a soft boiled or poached egg. Break up some dried Korean seaweed with your fingers and place it next to the poached egg.

TUNA POKE

Serves 2

Hawaiians adore this local rice bowl dish, which they call *ahi poke*. *Ahi* means "tuna" and *poke* means "sliced" or "cut", referring to the small pieces of fish scattered over the top of the rice. This refreshing and vibrant recipe, with a delicious, seasoned avocado and tuna topping served over cooled rice, is a perfect treat for a warm evening or weekend.

---

300 grams (10½ oz/1½ cups) japonica rice
1 fully ripe avocado
160 grams (5½ oz) very fresh, sashimi grade tuna, cubed
2 spring onions (scallions), stalk only, finely chopped

Marinade
2 tablespoons mirin
4 tablespoons Japanese soy sauce
1½ teaspoons sesame oil
1 teaspoon grated garlic
Pea-sized squeeze of wasabi paste
2 teaspoons white sesame seeds

1. Prepare your japonica rice according to the packet instructions (once ready, leave it to cool by spreading it on a wide plate, while you prepare the toppings for the dish).

2. Heat the mirin in a small pan to remove the alcohol, then allow to cool (you can, if you wish, omit this step). Cut the tuna into 1.5-cm (½-inch) cubes.

3. Mix the soy sauce, cooled mirin, sesame oil, wasabi, garlic, and sesame seeds in a bowl, add the raw tuna, mix well, and refrigerate for about 15 minutes to allow the flavours to blend and the tuna to cure.

4. Just prior to serving, peel, stone and cut the avocado into 1.5-cm (½-inch) cubes. Add the avocado to the cured tuna and spices and mix gently.

5. Divide the now-cooled rice between two bowls and serve the avocado and tuna mixture on top. Finish with a sprinkle of spring onions and sesame seeds.

COOKING TIPS

Tuna is lighter and more delicious when it is lean rather than fatty. If you find tuna that looks nearly red in colour, it tends to be the best quality, so be sure to give it a try.

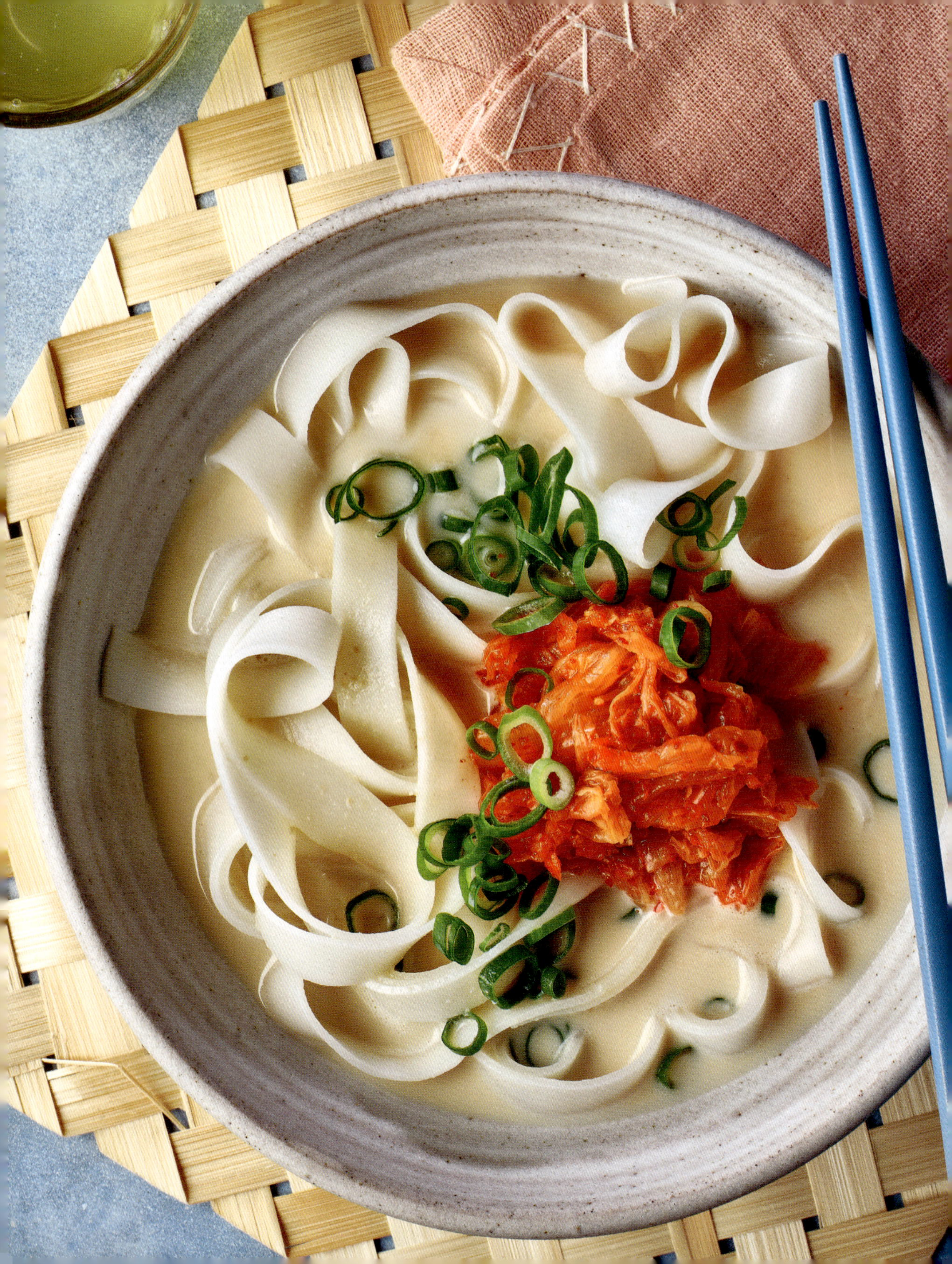

RICE NOODLES

Pho, pronounced "fuh", has become an integral part of Vietnamese culture and cuisine. It was first created at the turn of the 20th century, possibly under the influence of the French during their colonial times in Vietnam – *pho* may be a reference the French word *feu*, meaning "fire", over which the dish would be cooked. It rose in popularity, and by the 1950s it could be considered a national dish in Vietnam. *Banh pho* refers to the rice noodles that make the base of the dish and *pho* to the simple stew-like, one pot dish. The original recipe featured beef and was created in the Nam Dinh province, famed for the quality of its beef cattle. You can find *pho* throughout other East Asian cuisines, with Chinese, Cantonese and Thai versions being infamous for their fiery, spicy warmth. Vegetarian and vegan versions have been included here and, of course, with any of these recipes you can always swap out meat for your non-meat alternative of choice.

CHICKEN PHO

Serves 2

Chicken *pho* is the baby sibling of its more famous and original Vietnamese beef version. During the Vietnam War, soldiers and civilians alike would set up makeshift *pho* restaurants to enjoy a warm bowl of soup and escape the gloom of the war. Although it is easier to make than the beef version, it is just as aromatic and laden with warming ginger. Serve it topped with refreshing, fresh mint leaves for a deliciously satisfying, yet light meal.

---

120 grams (4 oz) skinless, boneless chicken breast
150 grams (5 oz) flat rice noodles
2 thumb-sized pieces of skin-on ginger, thinly sliced
800 ml (28 fl oz/3⅓ cups) water
1 tablespoon cooking sake
100 grams (3½ oz/1 cup) beansprouts
¼ teaspoon sugar
1½ tablespoons fish sauce
1 teaspoon chicken stock powder
Freshly ground pepper, 2–3 turns of the mill

Garnish
20 grams (½ oz/½ cup chopped) fresh coriander (cilantro), chopped into 3-cm (1¼-inch) lengths
2 tablespoons chopped spring onions (scallions)
Lime, cut into wedges
1 tablespoon dried fried onions
3–4 fresh mint leaves

1. Put the chicken, sliced ginger, water and sake into a pot over a medium-high heat and bring to a boil. Reduce the heat to low, cover and simmer for about 10 minutes, until the chicken is cooked through.

2. Remove the chicken, cover it with cling film (plastic wrap) to ensure it stays moist and allow to cool. Set aside the leftover cooking liquid. Once cool, cut the chicken into bite-sized strips about 5 mm (¼ inch) wide.

3. Cook the wide rice noodles in a separate saucepan of boiling water following the packet instructions. Immerse the beansprouts in a small sieve into the cooking water for 1 minute before the end of the noodles' cooking time. Drain the noodles and place them with the beansprouts in serving bowls.

4. Using the sieve, remove the ginger slices from the reserved chicken cooking liquid, then add the sugar, fish sauce, chicken stock powder and pepper to the stock. Bring to a boil to heat through.

5. Pour the soup over the noodles in the serving bowls and top with the chicken pieces, coriander and spring onions. Add lime, fried onions and mint leaves to garnish as desired.

RICE NOODLES

BEEF RICE NOODLES

Serves 2

Popular throughout the East, these beef noodles are called various names, depending on their origin; they are referred to as *pho bac* in Vietnam or *chow hor fun* going back to their Cantonese roots. One of the oldest beef noodle soups originated in north-west China and is known as *lanzhou lamian*. Whatever you call your rice noodles, this recipe is guaranteed to deliver a nourishing and tasty bowl.

---

150 grams (5 oz) flat rice noodles
200 grams (7 oz) rib or top sirloin (tenderloin) beef, cut into strips (shabu-shabu)
200 grams (7 oz/2¼ cups) beansprouts

Stock
1 packet dashi powder, mixed with 750 ml/1¼ pints/3 cups water
50 ml (1½ fl oz/scant ¼ cup) cooking sake
3½ tablespoons fish sauce
1 thumb of fresh root ginger (unpeeled), thinly sliced
1 clove garlic, crushed

Garnish
50 grams (2 oz) red onion
50 grams (2 oz/2 cups prepared) coriander (cilantro), leaves and stalks
1 lemon
8–10 fresh Thai basil leaves

1. Cook the flat rice noodles in a saucepan of boiling water following the packet instructions. Drain thoroughly and divide the noodles between two serving bowls. Quickly boil the beansprouts in the same water, drain and set aside.

2. Meanwhile, for the garnish, halve the red onion from root to top, cut it into thin slices, then soak the slices in water for 3 minutes and drain. Tear or snip the coriander leaves and stalks into bite-sized pieces. Cut the lemon in half horizontally.

3. For the soup stock, add the diluted dashi stock, sake, fish sauce, ginger slices and garlic to a pot over a medium heat. Once boiling, reduce the heat to low, cover and simmer for 5 minutes.

4. Fill another pot half-full of water and bring to the boil, then reduce it to a medium-low heat. Quickly dip the beef slices, one by one, into the simmering water for 20 seconds each. (Cooking them over a low heat will keep the meat tender.)

5. Place the beef slices on top of the rice noodles. Skim off any residue from the soup stock and pour the stock over the noodles and beef, then top with the beansprouts, red onion slices, basil and coriander leaves. When ready to eat, squeeze the lemon over the top and add more herb garnish as you eat.

PAD THAI

Serves 2

Unlike *pho*, pad Thai is a dry dish with crisply sautéed vegetables and meat and fragrant, seared aromatics. When adding the sauce and stir-frying, high heat and speed are important, so it's essential to prepare all of the ingredients you will be adding in advance. So that your rice noodles don't end up soggy, be sure to pat dry once soaked to get rid of excess water.

---

120 grams (4 oz) flat rice noodles
2 tablespoons vegetable oil
2 shallots or ½ small onion, thinly sliced
2 medium (US large) eggs, beaten
8 peeled prawns (shrimp)
10 grams (⅜ oz/¼ cup) dried shrimp
15 grams (½ oz/2 tablespoons) Takuan pickled yellow daikon (mooli), cut into 5-mm (¼-inch) cubes
20 grams (¾ oz) tofu, cut into 1.5-cm (½-inch) cubes and deep fried
10 grams (⅜ oz/¼ cup prepared) Chinese chives, cut into 4-cm (1¼-inch) lengths
60 grams (2 oz/⅔ cup) beansprouts

Seasoning sauce
70 grams (2½ oz/¼ cup) tamarind paste
80 grams (3 oz/¼ cup) coconut sugar
60 ml (2 fl oz/¼ cup) fish sauce

1. To make the seasoning sauce, put the tamarind paste, coconut sugar and fish sauce into a small saucepan over a medium heat and cook, stirring, for about 5 minutes. Remove from the heat. Set aside 2 tablespoons to season the noodles and store the remainder in a jar in the refrigerator for up to a month.

2. Soak the rice noodles in 20°C (68°F) warm water for 40 minutes. After soaking the noodles, wrap them in a cloth or kitchen paper towels and pat off excess water.

3. Heat the vegetable oil in a frying pan over a low heat, add the shallots or onion and fry until fragrant. Turn up the heat to high, pour in the beaten eggs all at once and stir roughly until they become fluffy and half-cooked.

4. Add in the rice noodles and continue to stir-fry over a high heat, then spoon over the reserved 2 tablespoons of the seasoning sauce.

5. Once the noodles are lightly coated with the sauce, add the peeled prawns, dried shrimp, pickled daikon, and deep-fried tofu, and stir-fry until the prawns are cooked through. Add the chives and beansprouts, turn off the heat, mix quickly and serve into bowls.

RICE NOODLES

PHO WITH PORK & COURGETTE CURRY

Serves 1

Pork (and prawn/shrimp) versions of *pho* are a newer alternative to beef varieties, and provide a lighter but still protein-rich way to enjoy this aromatic bowl of rice noodles. In many Eastern cultures, etiquette dictates that you should slurp your noodle broth to show appreciation and enjoyment. This recipe uses slim, round rice noodles.

---

60 grams (2 oz) pork belly
1½ tablespoons rice bran oil
25 grams (1 oz/⅓ medium) red bell pepper
100 grams (3 oz/1 small) courgette (zucchini)
50 grams (2 oz/½ medium) white onion
190 ml (6½ fl oz/¾ cup) water
50 grams (1¾ oz) rice vermicelli noodles
1 tablespoon chicken stock powder

Seasoning sauce
1 teaspoon curry powder
½ teaspoon oyster sauce
½ teaspoon dark soy sauce

1. Cut the pork belly into bite-sized pieces.
2. Deseed and slice the red pepper into thin strips, and cut the courgette in half lengthways and then slice into thin diagonal pieces. Slice the onion into thin strips.
3. For the seasoning sauce, mix the curry powder, oyster sauce and dark soy sauce together.
4. Heat ½ tablespoon of the rice bran oil in a frying pan over a medium heat. When hot, add the pork belly and fry until it changes colour. Now toss in the sliced vegetables and continue to fry until fragrant and tender.
5. Meanwhile, bring 190 ml (6½ fl oz/¾ cup) of water to the boil in a separate saucepan over a high heat, then turn down the heat to medium. Add the rice noodles and stir in the chicken stock powder. Cover and simmer over a medium heat for about 4 minutes (follow the packet instructions for the best results). Loosen the rice noodles gently with chopsticks halfway through.

6. Remove the lid, add the oyster sauce mixture to the noodles and fry the noodle and sauce mixture until the moisture has evaporated. Serve the sauce-coated noodles in a bowl and tip over the pork belly and vegetables.

PORK PHO CHINESE

Serves 2

Although beef is most commonly associated with Chinese pho, pork remains the more affordable protein option. In fact, it gained popularity in Asian cuisine after times of conflict, when beef became very expensive. This pho is reliably simple and stress-free but satisfyingly tasty.

150 grams (5¼ oz) minced (ground) pork
80 grams (3 oz/⅓ cup) zha cai (pickled Chinese mustard stalk)
1 teaspoon Japanese soy sauce
1 tablespoon cooking sake
2 tablespoons vegetable oil, plus extra for coating
2 medium (US large) eggs
¼ medium white onion, finely sliced
500 ml (17 fl oz/2 cups) water
4 pak choi (bok choy) leaves, sliced
90 grams (3 oz) flat rice noodles
2 teaspoons chicken stock powder
2–3 spring onions (scallions)
Pinch of salt

1. Lightly coat a medium-sized frying pan with oil (the pork will have enough fat to prevent it sticking) and heat it over a medium heat. Add the minced pork and *zha cai* and stir-fry until the pork turns a pale golden colour. Season with the soy sauce and sake and set aside on a plate.

2. Lightly wipe off the frying pan, then heat 2 tablespoons of oil in the same pan. Crack in and fry each egg, flipping them for an easy-over cook if you prefer, then remove them from the pan and set aside. Add the sliced onion to the remaining oil and stir-fry for 3–4 minutes until brown and caramelized.

3. In a separate pan, bring the water to the boil and add just the root sections of the pak choi for 30 seconds. After 30 seconds, add the rest of the pak choi leaves to the water and boil rapidly for 1 minute until tender. Remove the pak choi and set aside.

4. In the same water, add the noodles and simmer for 4 minutes (follow the packet instructions for the best results). When done, drain in a colander, saving 360 ml of the cooking water.

5. Divide the soy sauce and chicken stock powder equally between two bowls. Add a pinch of salt to each, then pour in 180 ml (6 fl oz/¾ cup) of the noodle cooking water to each bowl. Stir to make a dashi broth, then divide up the cooked noodles between each bowl. Top with pak choi, the minced meat, the fried onions, a fried egg and the spring onions.
6. Drizzle the burnt onion oil from the frying pan on top, for a sweetly caramelized drizzle.

THAI GREEN CURRY PHO NOODLES

Serves 2

Coconuts are offered at Thai temples as a symbol of purity and spiritual fulfilment, since coconut oil and coconut water are believed to have healing properties. Coconut milk is a staple in Thai cookery, chosen for its sweet flavour notes and the thickening, creamy effect it gives to curries. This curry *pho* is made with plenty of colourful vegetables. Use your favourite curry paste for this satisfying lunch or light supper dish.

---

300 grams (10½ oz) boneless, skinless chicken thighs
50 grams (2 oz/½ medium) white onion
40 grams (1½ oz/½ small) red bell pepper
20 grams (¾ oz/⅛ medium) lotus root
40 grams (1½ oz/¼ cup prepared) pumpkin
100 grams (3½ oz) flat rice noodles
Olive oil, to taste
2 tablespoons vegetable oil
25 grams (1 oz/2 tablespoons) Thai green curry paste
600 ml (1 pint/2½ cups) water
1½ tablespoons chicken stock powder
65 ml (2 fl oz/¼ cup) coconut milk
1 tablespoon Japanese soy sauce
2 tablespoons sugar
30 ml (1fl oz/2 tablespoons) fresh single (light) cream
Salt and pepper, to taste
2–3 spring onions (scallions), sliced, to garnish

1. Prepare the chicken thighs by removing the tendons and cutting the meat into bite-sized pieces. Cut the onion and red pepper into thin strips, and the lotus root and pumpkin into thin slices.

2. Cook the noodles in a saucepan of boiling water for around 4 minutes (follow the packet instructions for the best results), then drain in a colander and cool under cold water. Drain thoroughly and toss with a small amount of olive oil.

3. Heat the vegetable oil in a pot over a medium heat and when sizzling add the lotus root and pumpkin. Fry until browned, then remove the vegetables from the pot and set aside. Now add the chicken thigh pieces to the same pot and fry until golden brown, then add the sliced onion and red pepper and fry for a further 3–4 minutes until the onion softens. Scoop in the Thai curry paste and sauté for 2 to 3 minutes until fragrant and aromatic.

4. Pour the water into the same pot and mix in the chicken stock powder, coconut milk, soy sauce and sugar. Bring the cooking liquid to a simmer, and simmer for around 4 minutes until the chicken is cooked through. Add the lotus root and pumpkin back in.

5. Add the flat rice noodles to the curry and stir in the fresh cream with a little salt and pepper to taste. Serve in deep bowls, topped with the spring onions.

MISO MILK KIMCHI PHO

Serves 2

This soothing, aromatic milky broth has its roots in Thai cooking, but it replaces coconut milk with a miso-flavoured milk for its broth. It has the added zing of fermented kimchi, which is renowned for its gut-healing properties. It requires very few ingredients and makes a perfect lunchtime snack or a light healthy supper, when you don't have the energy for complicated or lengthy cooking.

---

160 grams (5½ oz) flat rice noodles
300 ml (10½ fl oz/1¼ cups) milk
200 ml (7 fl oz/scant 1 cup) chicken stock
2 tablespoons miso paste
60 grams (2½ oz/¼ cup) kimchi, roughly chopped into smaller pieces
2–3 spring onions (scallions), thinly sliced
Salt and pepper, to taste

See the chapter opener for this recipe's image.

1. Cook the flat rice noodles in a saucepan of boiling water for around for 4 minutes (follow the packet instructions for the best results). Drain and set aside.

2. In a separate pan, combine the milk with the chicken stock liquid (make up 200 ml/7 fl oz/scant 1 cup with chicken stock powder or chicken stock/bouillion cubes) and bring to a boil. Spoon in the miso paste, taste the broth and adjust to your liking with salt and pepper.

3. After about 2 minutes, add the kimchi to the broth and bring it back to a boil. Now divide the noodles between serving bowls, pour over the tangy broth and sprinkle over the spring onion slices.

SPICY PHO

Serves 2

Slightly spicy and enlivening! This is a reproduction of what the Chinese sometimes refer to as their soul food, so-called for the smooth and chewy noodles that are made for a mindful, meditative eating experience. This recipe allows you to fully enjoy the aroma and smoky, woody flavours of inky black Chinese vinegar and will be a must-make for those who like sour food notes.

---

140 grams (5 oz) flat rice noodles
200 grams (7 oz) minced (ground) pork
Dried chilli pepper strands, to garnish
1 teaspoon tenmenjiang (sweet bean sauce)

Seasoned dressing
2–3 spring onions (scallions), finely chopped
4 teaspoons dried fried onion
1 teaspoon Chinese black vinegar
½ teaspoon sesame oil
½ teaspoon chilli oil
½ teaspoon chilli powder
½ teaspoon ground Japanese pepper

Sauce
2½ teaspoons chilli oil
20 grams (¾ oz) zha cai (pickled vegetables)
2 teaspoons sesame paste or tahini
1½ teaspoons Japanese soy sauce
2 teaspoons just-boiled water

1. Prepare the seasoned dressing by combining the spring onions, fried onion, black vinegar, sesame oil, chilli oil, chilli powder and powdered Japanese pepper in a small bowl.

2. Cook the flat rice noodles in a saucepan of boiling water, following the packet instructions. Remove the noodles from the liquid, drain through a colander and reserve the cooking water, which will be used later. Set the noodles aside.

3. Fry the minced pork in a frying pan over a medium heat; when the liquid has evaporated, tip the fried mince onto some kitchen paper towels and pat away any excess oil before placing it in a bowl. Add in the sweet bean sauce and mix together well.

4. Put the chili oil, *zha cai*, sesame paste (or tahini), soy sauce and boiled water into a bowl and mix well to make an emulsified sauce. Tip in the boiled noodles and mix well.

5. Divide the sauce-tossed noodles between bowls and fork the pork mince over them, before drizzling over the seasoned dressing. Add extra spice to your dish by sprinkling with chilli strands.

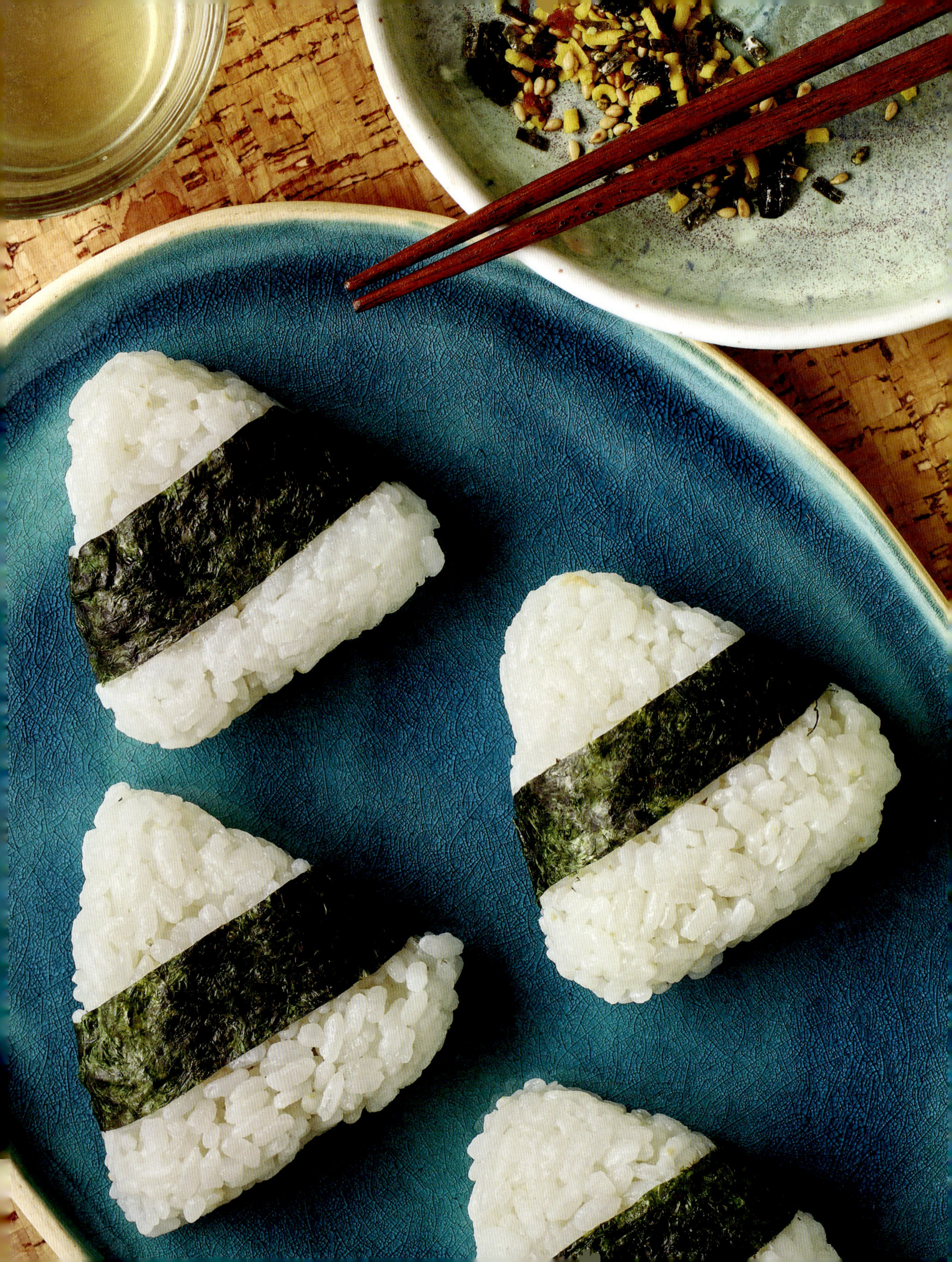

ONIGIRI, BREAKFASTS & MORE

The recipes in this chapter are full of inspiring ideas for snacks, breakfasts and simple rice meals. One such snack is *onigiri*. Also known as *omusubi*, or rice balls, *onigiri* are tasty balls of rice that have become a huge trend in recent years, with destination stores in Japan selling nothing but these tasty bites. Filled with savoury or tangy fillings – often smoked salmon or pickles – they are triangular or cylindrical in shape, making them super portable, healthy, protein-rich snacks when you are on the go.

CHEESE ONIGIRI

Makes 4 onigiri

Over recent times, dairy produce has been used increasingly in Asian dishes, but this wasn't always the case. Although curdled milks and butters can be traced back to ancient times, it wasn't until World War II that the Japanese really started to embrace cheese. Now the country imports vast quantities of cheese, beloved for its salty, creamy taste, and artisanal cheese producers can be found all over Japan.

---

480 grams (17 oz/2½ cups) cooked japonica rice
40 grams (1½ oz/generous ⅓ cup) grated mozzarella cheese or Cheddar cheese
2 tablespoons sesame oil

Soy sauce coating
3 tablespoons Japanese soy sauce
3 tablespoons mirin
1 teaspoon shichimi togarashi spice blend (optional)

1. Put the soy sauce, mirin and *shichimi togarashi* into a small bowl and mix well.

2. Wet your hands a little and sprinkle them with salt. Now take one quarter of the cooked rice and place it in your palm. Make a slight indentation into the middle of the rice and pop 10 grams (⅜ oz/1½ tablespoons) of cheese into it, then seal it in by covering it with the plain rice from around the edges.

3. Form the rice into a 3D triangular shape and squeeze it gently to ensure the cheese is sealed in and there are no gaps. Make 4 of these triangles, using up all of the rice and cheese.

4. Heat the sesame oil in a frying pan over a medium heat. Gently place each triangle into it with a flat side down, then, using a pastry brush, coat the upward facing sides with the soy sauce mixture.

5. Fry the triangles for about 1 minute until they are golden, then turn them over and coat the unseasoned side with the mix. Repeat this process, brushing them with the soy sauce coating until they are golden brown on both sides.
6. Serve on a plate and enjoy.

HOW TO SHAPE ONIGIRI

Place a small ball of cooked rice (about 80 grams/3 oz/⅓ cup) in one hand. To add a filling, make a depression in the centre of the ball, add your chosen ingredients and cover it up by squeezing the rice gently around it. Make a cupped "U" shape with your other hand and gently rotate the rice ball to make the classic *onigiri* triangular shape, squeezing the rice gently into shape. When squeezing, take care not to use too much pressure.

ONIGIRI, BREAKFASTS & MORE

GIANT ONIGIRI SANDWICH

Serves 1

When more is better! This supersized sandwich subtly alters the ratio of rice, filling and seaweed wrap layer to deliver a satisfying all-in-one lunchbox. Once you have mastered the technique, feel free to experiment with the fillings. Chicken, cruciferous veg (such as broccoli and cabbage) and marinated tofu are all good options. If you make extra rice, you can store it (see page 16) and any extra filling, so you can make fresh *onigiri* sandwiches for a couple of days. They are best assembled daily to keep that freshness, so apply the seaweed wrapper on the day of eating.

---

200 grams (7 oz/1 cup) cooked japonica rice
Drizzle of vegetable oil
1 medium (US large) egg
1 sheet nori seaweed
2 cos lettuce leaves

Tuna filling
50 grams (1½ oz) canned tuna
2 tablespoons mayonnaise
1 teaspoon Japanese soy sauce
Pinch of salt
Freshly ground black pepper (2–3 turns of the mill)

1. Drain the canned tuna well and tip it into a small bowl. Now add in the mayonnaise, soy sauce, salt and pepper and mix well. Taste and adjust the seasoning as desired.

2. Heat the vegetable oil in a frying pan over low-medium heat and fry the egg on both sides, then let it cool a little. Once the egg has slightly cooled, take the sheet of nori seaweed and place it on a chopping board covered with a sheet of cling film (plastic wrap).

3. Time to build the sandwich. Spread the cooked rice over the middle of the nori, leaving a border round the rice to fold the seaweed sheet over the contents. Now lay one of the cos lettuce leaves over the rice. Top the lettuce leaf with the tuna mayo mixture and then the fried egg; put the remaining lettuce leaf on top of the egg.

4. Now fold all four corners of the nori seaweed sheet toward the centre, one by one. Wrap it in the cling film and allow the nori to settle (it needs to absorb a little moisture from the rice to soften slightly).

5. After 5 minutes or so, remove the clingfilm and cut the onigiri sandwich in half down the middle to reveal the layered filling and enjoy.

ONIGIRI, BREAKFASTS & MORE

AROMATIC RICE SOUP

Serves 2

This recipe requires the flavouring ingredients to infuse and marinate overnight. Super simple, it is based on an *ochazuke* recipe, which is rice and green tea. It takes little effort, other than some forward thinking. The result is the most amazing, nutrient-rich, savoury, soupy, rice porridge, which takes just minutes to prepare in the morning, as the fridge has done all the hard work.

300 grams (10½ oz/1½ cups) cooked japonica rice
12 grams (scant ¾ oz/2 tablespoons) sencha tea leaves
360 ml (12½ fl oz/1½ cups) boiling water

Dashi stock
600 ml (1 pint/2½ cups) cold water
5 grams (¼ oz/scant 3 tablespoons) kombu (edible kelp)
10 grams (½ oz/3/4 cup) dried bonito flakes

1. The night before, to make the *dashi* stock, fill a bowl with the cold water and drop in your *kombu*. Cover it with cling film (plastic wrap), pop it in the fridge and leave overnight to infuse.

2. In the morning, pour the infused liquid into a saucepan and heat it over a high heat until it comes to the boil. Once it starts to boil, remove the *kombu*, then sprinkle in the bonito flakes and turn off the heat. Allow the flakes to marinate in the hot water for about 5 minutes, then strain through a sieve, reserving the liquid.

3. Put your cooked rice into two serving bowls. Put the sencha tea leaves into a teapot or similar, pour in the boiling water and let infuse for about 2 minutes.

4. Combine the sencha tea with the dashi stock and pour over the rice in each bowl.

ONIGIRI, BREAKFASTS & MORE

EASY RICE PORRIDGE

Serves 1

For those who are keen to avoid oat-based porridges containing gluten, this authentic Japanese version offers a tasty and addictive alternative. You will find yourself making it for a warming, fuss-free breakfast in winter that will keep you sated until lunchtime. For an even slower release option, try using brown rice (adjusting the cooking time to allow for the coarser grain to breakdown and soften).

60 grams (2 oz/⅓ cup) japonica rice
600 ml (1 pint/ 2½ cups) water
2 pinches of salt

1. Put the measured-out rice into a bowl and wash it. After pouring in water once, drain it quickly. Since there is only a small amount of rice, lightly rub it with your fingertips (about 10 times) to wash it, then change the water several times and drain it.
2. Put the rice into a saucepan and pour in the specified amount of water.
3. Place the saucepan over a medium heat. Just before the liquid boils, the surface will start to turn white – but do not do anything to the rice. Only when it starts to boil, gently stir the rice once or twice with a spoon to prevent the rice sticking to the bottom of the pan. As soon as the pan is boiling, turn down the heat to low and cover with a lid, leaving a gap large enough to hold a chopstick.
4. Keep the heat on low and cook for 30–40 minutes without stirring.
5. Once it has reached the desired consistency, which is quite liquid-y and soft, like rice pudding (making it easily digestible), remove the rice porridge from the heat and add two pinches of salt. Mix gently and it's ready to eat.

FRAGRANT DASHI RICE WITH FISH

Serves 1

Sea bream is a lean, non-oily fish with dense flesh and a rich flavour. Here it is "cured" in vinegar, a process called *kinilaw* in the Philipines and *ceviche* in Peru. Paired with dashi stock, it enhances the fish and adds additional umami flavour. Dashi can be made of *kombu* (kelp seaweed), *katsuobushi* (bonito or dried smoked fish flakes) or shiitake mushrooms. It is used as the base of miso soups and is a great addition to many Japanese-inspired dishes. You can purchase dashi ready-made in good supermarkets and it is a handy, store-cupboard staple.

200 grams (7 oz/1 cup) cooked japonica rice
2–3 stalks mitsuba (Japanese parsley) or flat leaf parsley
50 grams (1½ oz) sashimi-grade sea bream fillets
Pea-sized amount of wasabi root or squeeze of wasabi paste
250 ml (8 fl oz/1 cup) dashi stock

Sesame sauce
1½ tablespoons white sesame seeds or white sesame seed paste
2 teaspoons dark soy sauce
½ teaspoon mirin

1. After cooking the rice (see page 14), tip it into a small bowl to remain warm. Finely chop the *mitsuba* or parsley.
2. Grind the white sesame seeds in a pestle and mortar. If you don't have a mortar, you can use 10 grams (scant ½ oz/2 teaspoons) white sesame paste or 1 tablespoon of ground sesame seeds. Combine the soy sauce, ground sesame and mirin to make a sesame sauce.
3. Lay your sea bream fillet on a plate. Slice it widthways and coat the slices with the sesame sauce. Set aside and allow to cure for about 5 minutes.
4. Top the cooked rice with the cured sea bream and *mitsuba*.
5. Grate a pea-sized amount of the wasabi root or squeeze it out of the tube. Heat the dashi stock in a small saucepan until it is just bubbling, mix in half the wasabi, then pour it over the sea bream and rice. Smudge the other half of the wasabi on the side of each bowl, and it's ready.

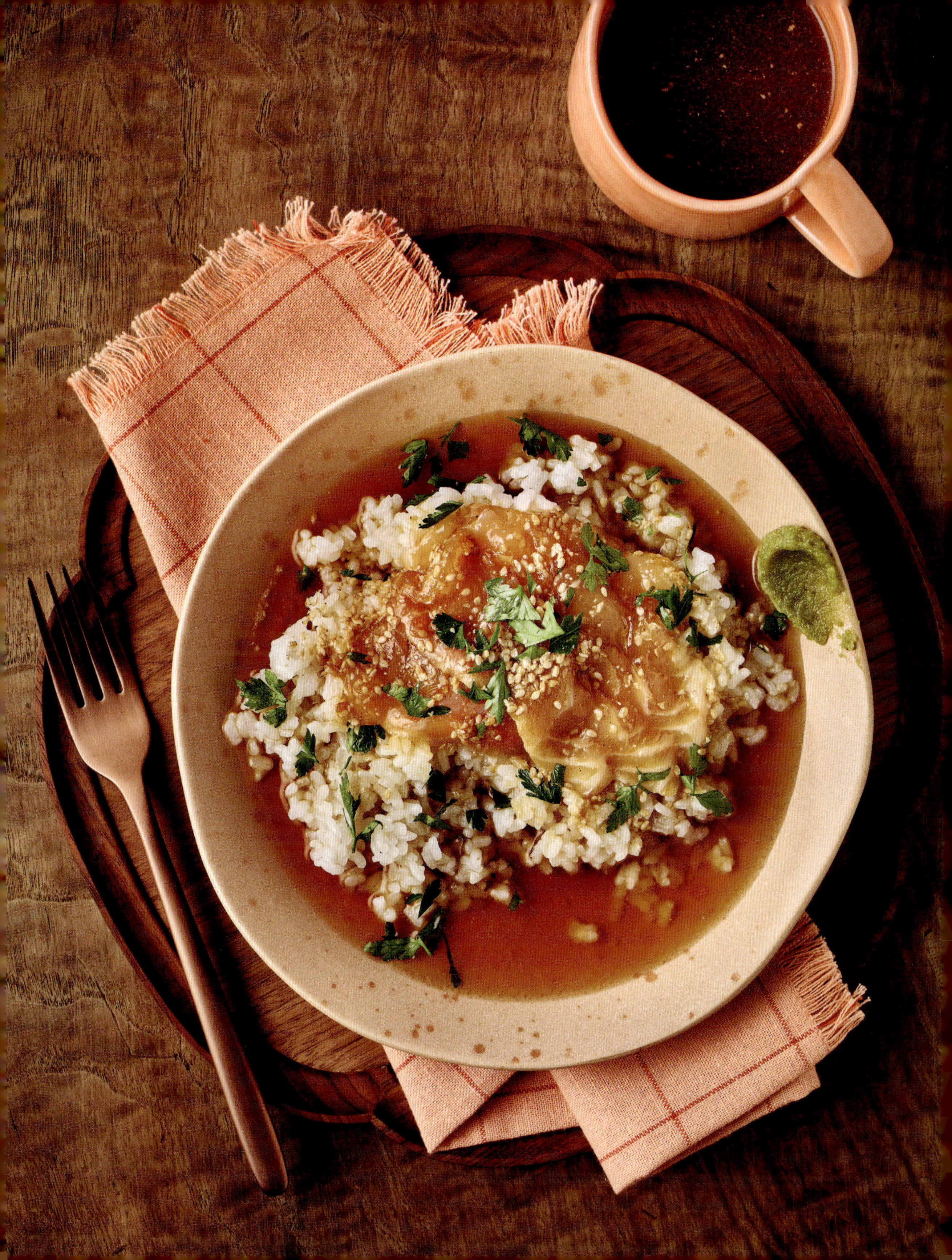

TEMPURA ONIGIRI

Makes 2 onigir

Forget the heavy batter of traditional fish and chips and sample instead the light crunch of tempura. From the Latin meaning "time", tempura is a method of swiftly deep-frying seafood and vegetables to create an air-light finish. In this dish, the carb of chips is replaced with rice, and the green of mushy peas is transformed into the dark green, vitamin- and mineral-rich bite of dried nori seaweed.

---

100 grams (3½ oz/½ cup) cooked japonica rice
Pinch of salt
2 whole prawns (shrimp) in their shells
2 tablespoons tempura flour
2 tablespoons cold water
300 ml (10 fl oz/1¼ cups) vegetable oil
1 tablespoon chicken soup stock (*mentsuyu*), double concentrated
2 sheets (18 x 5 cm/7 x 2 inches) dried nori seaweed
2 fresh shiso (perilla) leaves

1. After cooking the rice (see page 14), add a pinch of salt, mix gently through and set the pan aside so the rice becomes warm, not piping hot.
2. Remove the shells from the prawns down to the tail end, leaving the tail tip. Using a sharp knife, make a slit down the back to remove the black vein. Score the underside of each prawn slightly.
3. Heat the vegetable oil to 180°C (350°F). Mix the tempura flour and cold water in a small bowl to make a smooth batter.
4. Dip the prawns into the tempura batter to coat, then deep-fry the coated prawns in the hot oil. When the prawns are crispy, remove them from the oil with a slotted spoon and place them on kitchen paper towels to drain away the excess oil.
5. Now dip the bottom half of the prawns into the concentrated chicken stock.
6. Place each nori seaweed sheet on a piece of clingfilm (plastic wrap). Divide the rice into two equal portions, then spread

half of each sheet with a portion of the cooked rice. Place a tempura prawn on each and wrap the nori seaweed and cling film round the rice and prawns to make cylinders, pressing gently so they are firm. Allow them to sit for a few minutes to take on their shape and become a little soft, then remove the cling film. Garnish with the shiso leaves to finish.

ONIGIRI, BREAKFASTS & MORE

MIZUNA & SALMON RICE TEA

Serves 2

Either wild or cultivated, mizuna is a feathery leafed, Japanese salad vegetable that is akin to rocket (arugula), with a slight hint of peppery, mustardy notes. It is a cut-and-come-again leaf that you can grow quite easily on a windowsill or in garden vegetable patch. It cuts through the richness of salmon, creating a balanced, flavoursome and light dish, perfect as a lunchtime meal.

---

300 grams (10½ oz/1½ cups) cooked japonica rice
1 salmon fillet
1 tablespoon salt
¼ bag mizuna leaves or rocket (arugula)
1½ teaspoons sesame oil
White sesame seeds, to sprinkle

Dashi stock
Pinch of salt
300 ml (10 fl oz/1¼ cups) water
1 teaspoon kelp powder

1. After putting the rice on to cook (see page 14), once softened, let it sit in the pan; it should still be slightly liquid-y (this dish is a slightly soupy rice). Slice the salmon fillet into bite-sized pieces and sprinkle with plenty of salt. Cut the mizuna into bite-sized pieces.

2. Heat the sesame oil in a frying pan over a medium heat, add the salted salmon strips and sauté for a few minutes until browned.

3. For the dashi stock, add the salt, water and kelp powder to a small saucepan and bring to a boil. Stir quickly for 3 minutes, then turn off the heat.

4. Spoon your cooked rice into two serving bowls. Top with the sautéed salmon and shredded mizuna leaves, then pour your dashi stock over and sprinkle with white sesame seeds.

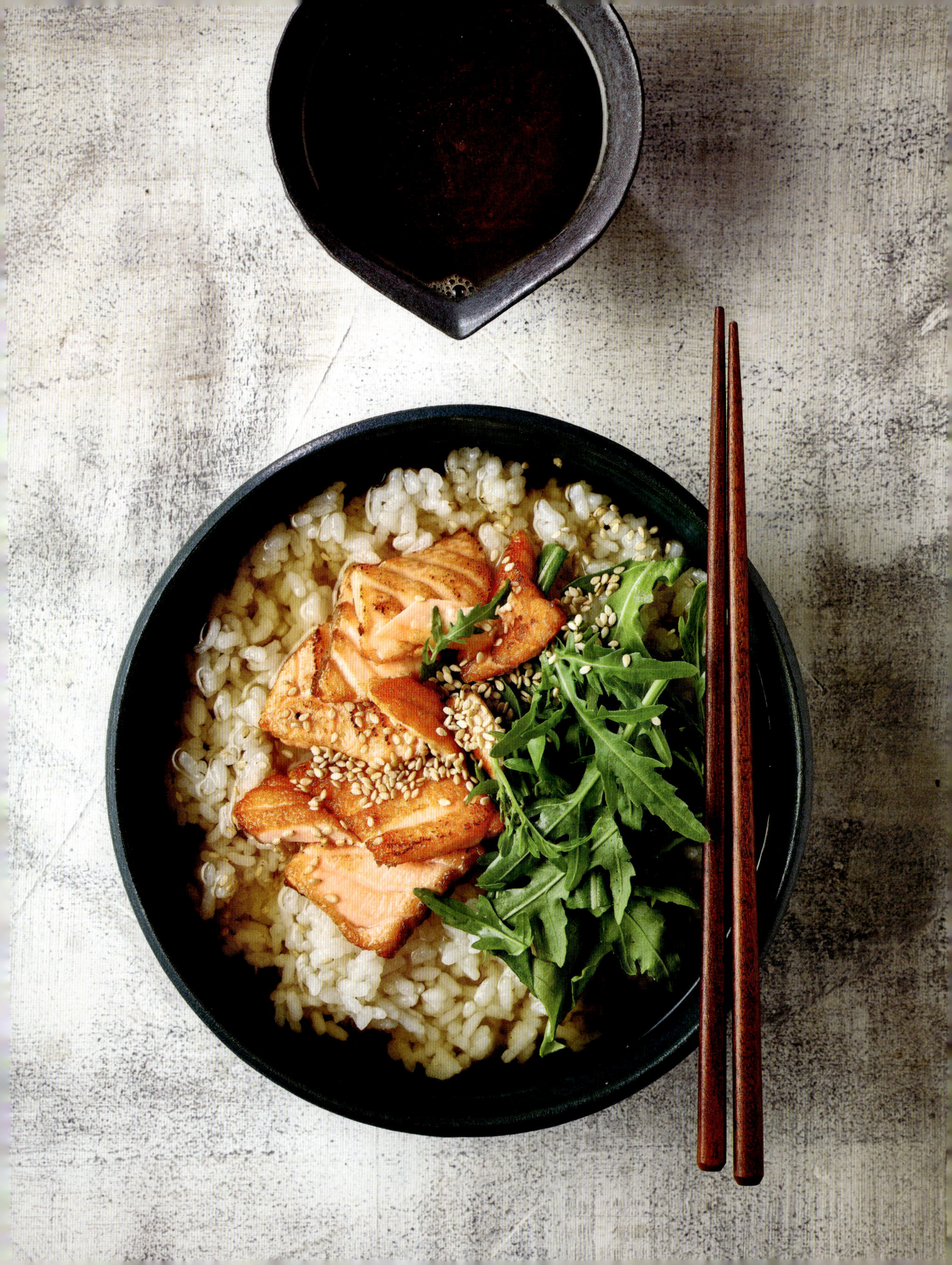

SEA CHICKEN MAYO ONIGIRI

Makes 6 onigiri

"Sea chicken" is the colloquial Japanese name for canned tuna. This term came about in part as tuna is plentiful, but also because it was how fishermen would refer to a specific type of white albacore tuna, which had very pale flesh and a mild flavour reminiscent of chicken. Mayonnaise is a modern addition to these traditional onigiri bites.

300g (10½ oz/1½ cups) cooked japonica rice
Pinch of salt
1 x 70 gram (2½ oz) can of tuna
¼ white onion, finely chopped
1 teaspoon salted butter
1 teaspoon Japanese soy sauce
1 teaspoon mayonnaise
Slightly roasted nori seaweed (½ size sheets)

1. After cooking the rice (see page 14), add a pinch of salt, mix gently through and set the pan aside so the rice becomes warm, not piping hot.

2. Drain the canned tuna and use a fork to break it up the chunks into flakes.

3. Put the onion into a bowl, place the butter on top and microwave (600W) for 2 minutes; alternatively, melt the butter in a small saucepan over a medium heat, add the onion and cook for a few minutes until softened.

4. Add the tuna flakes, soy sauce and mayo to the softened onion and melted butter and mix.

5. Divide the rice into 6 equal portions and place them on a sheet of cling film (plastic wrap), in little mounds. Make a well in the middle of each mound and add the tuna filling, dividing it equally between all of the rice mounds. Seal in the tuna filling by pushing the outer rice round the filling and squeezing lightly.

6. Wrap a strip of nori seaweed round each rice ball to finish the *onigiri*, and enjoy.

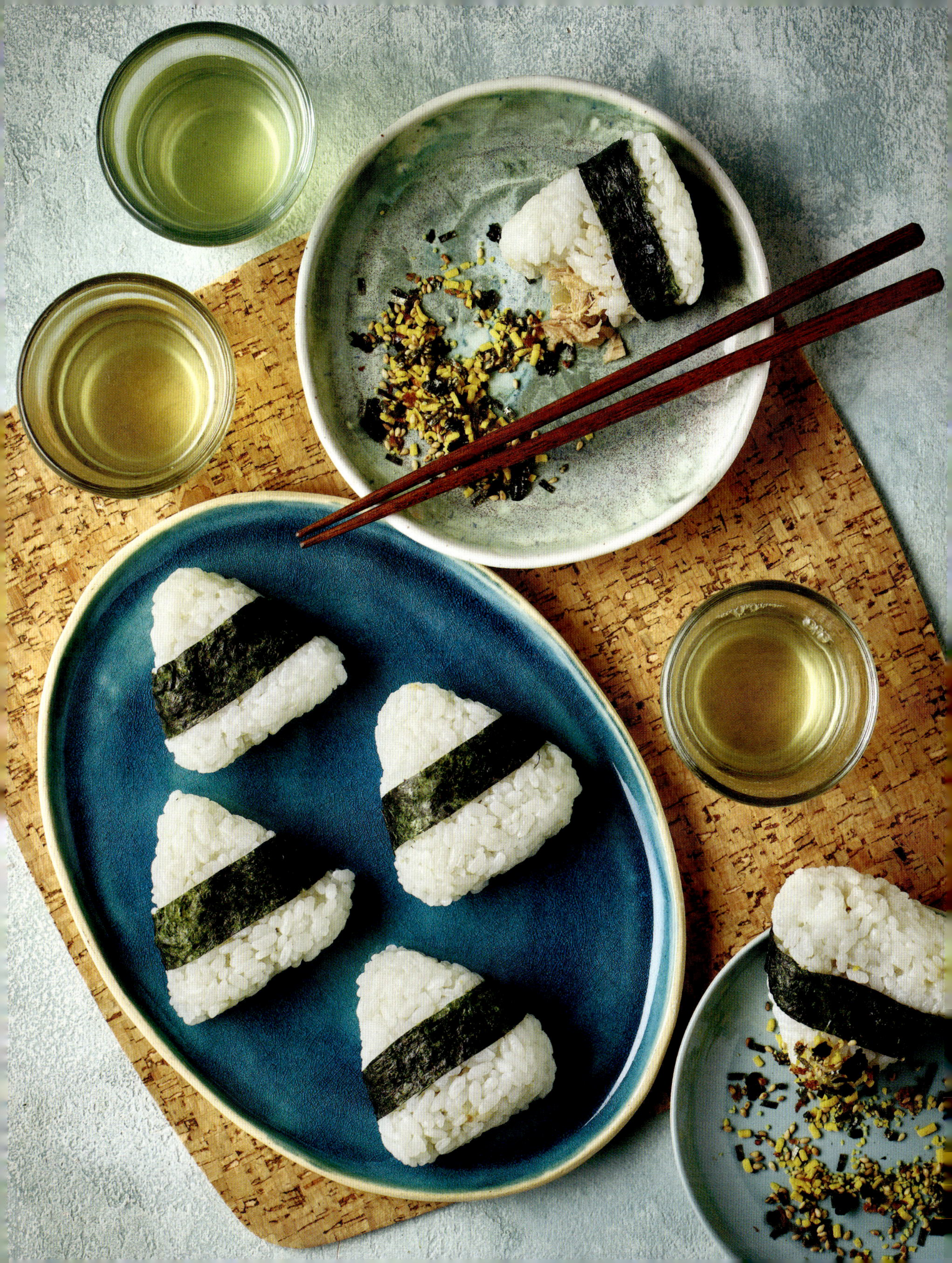

SALMON WITH GREEN TEA CHAZUKE

Serves 2

Chazuke, or *ochazuke*, is also known as *bubuzuke* in the historic Japanese city of Kyoto. A super-simple Japanese dish, it is made by pouring green tea or dashi stock – or even just salted hot water – over cooked rice. It is a super-fast way to create a quick snack or speedy lunch, and it is also the perfect way to use up leftover rice. Because it is so easy to make and requires few ingredients, it is also very cost effective. Of course, you can add any toppings you desire to make it your own. Here, I have raised the bar by adding in deliciously nutritious salted salmon.

---

300 grams (10½ oz/1½ cups) cooked rice
80 grams (3 oz) salmon fillet
2 tablespoons sea salt
Drizzle of vegetable oil
1 heaped teaspoon green tea (tea leaves)
400 ml (14 fl oz/1 ⅔ cups) boiling water

Garnish
1 tablespoon chopped spring onion (scallion)
Dried seaweed, broken up into shards
1 teaspoon white sesame seeds

1. After cooking the rice following the packet instructions, set the pan aside so the rice becomes warm, not piping hot. Alternatively, use any leftover rice that has been properly stored.

2. Sprinkle the salmon with the sea salt, massaging it over well, then wrap the salmon in cling film (plastic wrap) and refrigerate for an hour.

3. Once chilled, heat the vegetable oil in a frying pan over a medium heat, add the salmon, skin side down, and cook it for 3 minutes until golden brown. Turn it over, cover the pan with a lid and cook for a further 3 minutes until the fish is cooked through, then let it cool. Once cooled, remove the skin, which should come away easily, and any fine bones from the salmon, and break the flesh into largish pieces.

4. Put the green tea leaves and boiling water into a teapot, cover and allow to brew for about 2 minutes.

5. Put your cooked or leftover rice in two bowls, place the flaked salted salmon on top, and sprinkle with the chopped spring onion, broken shards of dried seaweed, and white sesame seeds. Pour the green tea infusion over it and enjoy.

ONIGIRI, BREAKFASTS & MORE

MUSSELS & WASABI WITH ROASTED GREEN TEA

Serves 2

Here is another super-simple take on the *chazuke* style of enjoying rice. This one adds a few extra delicacies to elevate the recipe for the perfect light supper, yet it retains its authentic, green tea flavours. Feel free to experiment with any leftovers you may have to top or add to your rice bowl. The no-wasted food principle really applies to this style of cooking.

---

300 grams (10½ oz/1½ cups) cooked japonica rice
400 ml (14 fl oz/1 ⅔ cups) water
1 roasted green tea teabag (*hoji* tea)
¼ teaspoon grated ginger
1 can or jar of mussels
1 teaspoon wasabi paste
3 spring onions (scallions), thinly sliced
4 tablespoons dried seaweed

1. After cooking the rice following the packet instructions, set the pan aside so the rice becomes warm, not piping hot. Alternatively, use any leftover rice that has been properly stored (see page 16).

2. Put the water into a saucepan over a high heat and bring it to the boil. When it boils, turn off the heat, add the roasted green tea teabag and allow it to infuse for 1 minute. Remove the teabag and add in the grated ginger, stirring it through the liquid.

3. Divide the cooked rice between 2 serving bowls and add half the mussels on top of each. Place ½ teaspoon of wasabi paste on top of each, then pour over the warm green tea and ginger broth. Sprinkle with the sliced spring onions, then break shards of dried seaweed over the top and mix each bowl and its contents well before serving.

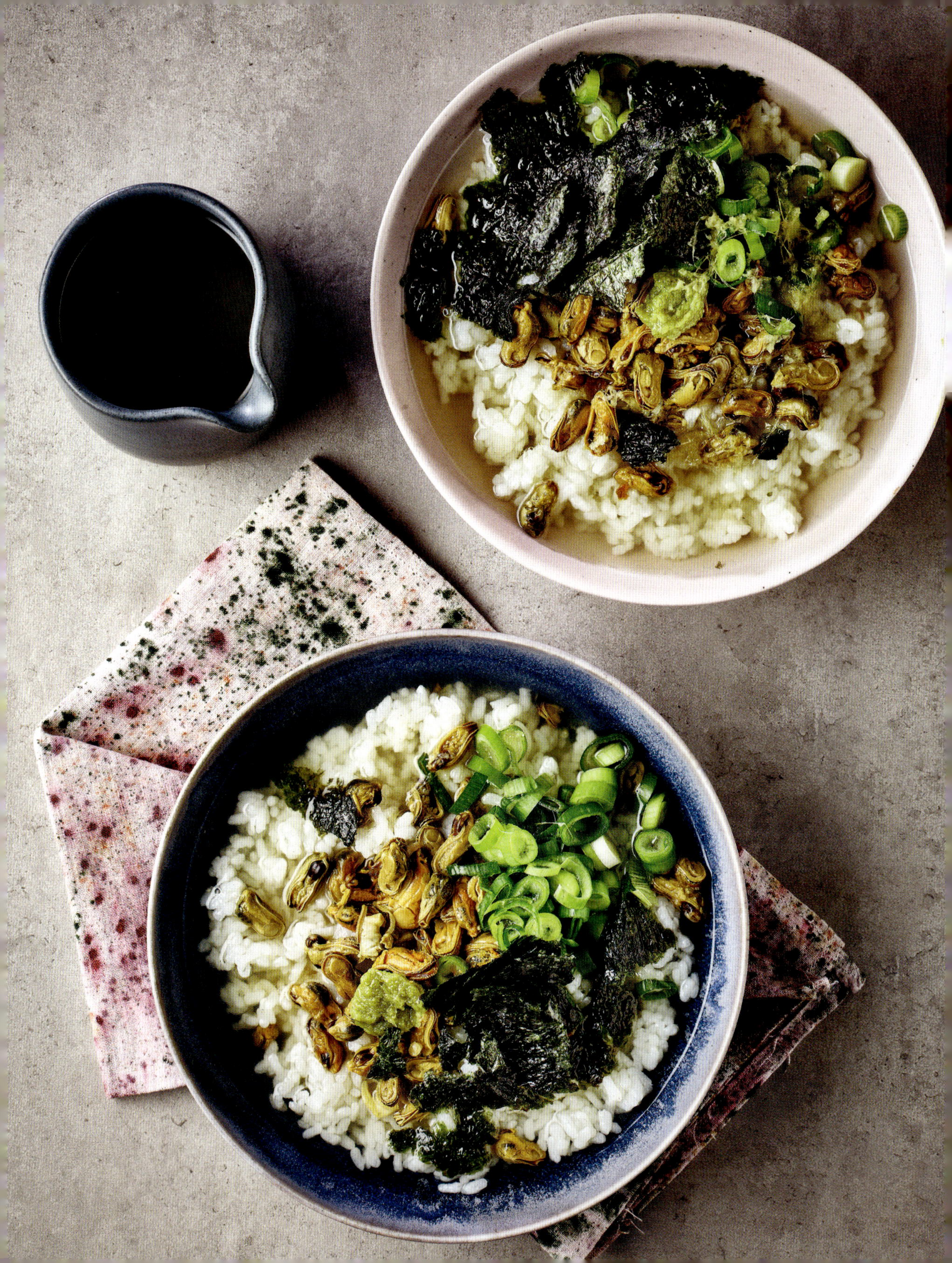

COCONUT MANGO RICE

Serves 2 as a dessert

You can think of this as a bit like a traditional British rice pudding. Known in Japan as *sho-chiku-bai*, the rice for this dish is sticky and super-starchy, which gives this pudding an unctuous, glutinous texture. The sweetness of the mango cuts through the richness of the dish, making it a perfect spring dessert. The secret to perfect sticky rice is to soak the rice in a pan of water for about 3 hours, so allow time to do this in advance of preparing the dish.

---

80 grams (3 oz/½ cup) sticky (glutinous) rice
1 whole mango
200 ml (7 fl oz/scant 1 cup) coconut milk
300 ml (10 fl oz/1¼ cups) condensed milk
2 teaspoons sugar
¼ teaspoon salt
½ teaspoon cornflour (cornstarch)
White sesame seeds or other toppings of your choice, to garnish

1. Rinse the rice well under running water in a sieve, then soak it in a saucepan of water for about 3 hours.

2. Once soaked, drain the rice and put it into a steamer basket over a saucepan of water on a high heat (the classic method for cooking this type of rice). After the water boils, turn the heat down and steam for about 20 minutes until the rice looks sticky and translucent. You can adjust the cooking time to your liking.

3. In the meantime, peel and stone the mango, then cut the flesh into slices.

4. Now make a sauce by putting the coconut milk, condensed milk, sugar, salt and cornflour into a saucepan over a medium heat, and when it begins to simmer, turn the heat down to low – stir continuously and take care it doesn't burn. When the sugar is fully dissolved and the mixture seems creamy in consistency, turn off the heat.

5. Serve the steamed rice on two plates and pour over as much of the sauce as you like. Garnish with the sliced, peeled mango and sprinkle with white sesame seeds or other toppings of your choice.

ONIGIRI, BREAKFASTS & MORE

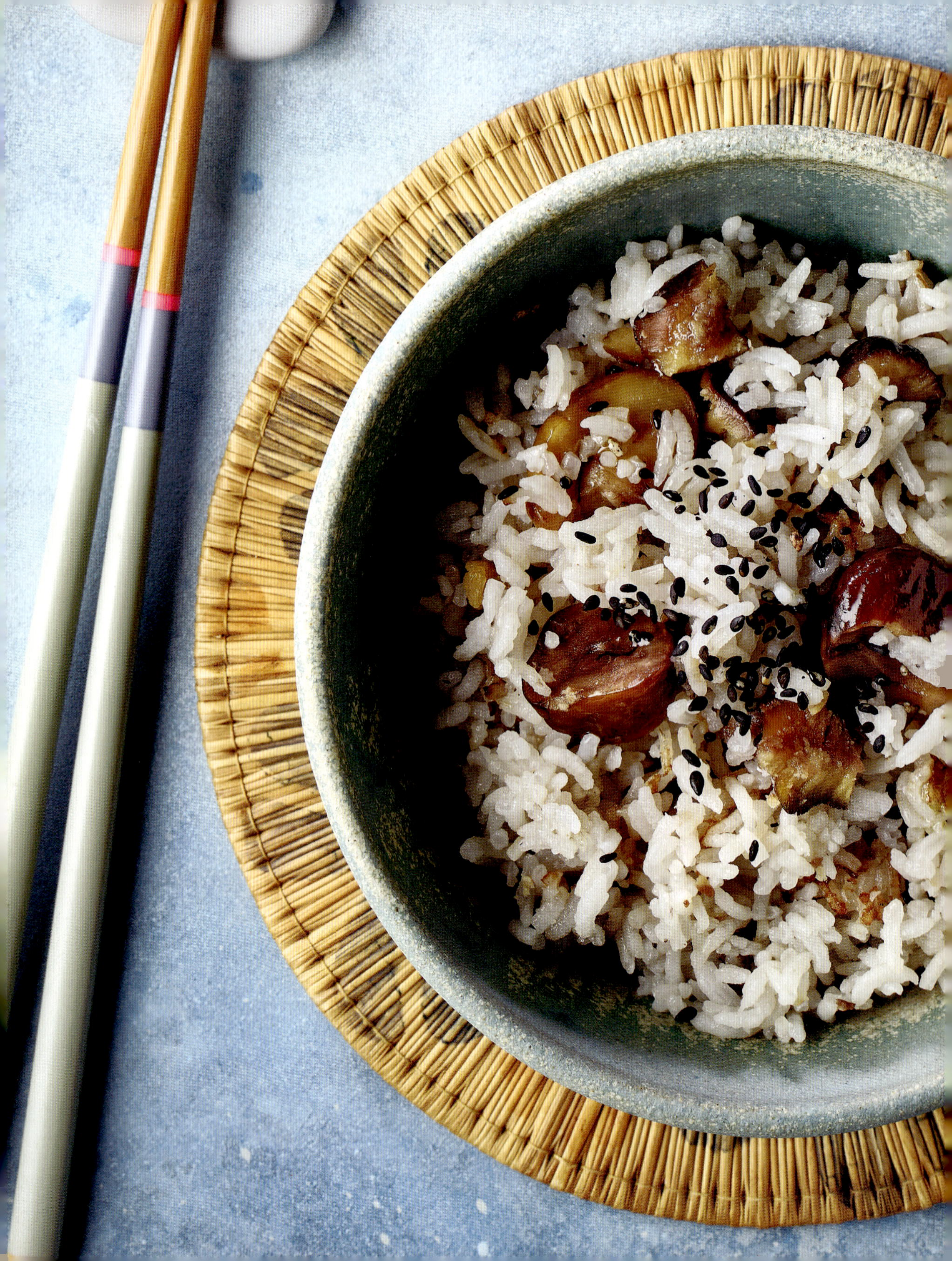

RICE COOKER DISHES

In the last few years, we have embraced slow cookers and air fryers, nifty gadgets that allow us to prepare fuss-free meals and save energy as we go. In Asia, they have been utilizing the foolproof and equally time-saving rice cooker. Once you have tried this gadget, you will be a fan: it produces perfect rice every time, including sticky rice, for those craving its gooey chew. But that's not all. Just like a slow cooker, with a little prep you can create delicious rice meals in just a few steps. Rice cookers use a cup measurement (they come with the rice cooker cup) with markings in the internal pot to help you fill water to the correct level every time. Just follow these short and sweet recipes in this chapter.

NO-FAIL STICKY RICE

Serves 3

There are thousands of varieties of sticky rice, and recipes for this ingredient can be found in ancient texts throughout Asia. If this is something you haven't tried cooking before, then it is well worth attempting – albeit the unctuous results take just a little practice to perfect in or with this style of rice. This recipe is foolproof.

3 rice cooker cups sticky (glutinous) rice
4 dried shiitake mushrooms
50 ml (1½ fl oz/scant ¼ cup) warm water, to rehydrate the mushrooms
200 grams (7 oz) pork belly
2 tablespoons cooking sake
2 tablespoons Japanese soy sauce
2 cloves garlic
1 tablespoon olive oil
1–2 spring onions (scallions), finely chopped (optional), to garnish
Sesame seeds (optional), to garnish

Rice
3 tablespoons cooking sake
2½ tablespoons Japanese soy sauce
2 teaspoons chicken stock powder
½ teaspoon salt
2 teaspoons sugar
1 teaspoon Chinese five-spice powder
130 ml (4¼ fl oz/generous ½ cup) cold water

1. Rinse your rice thoroughly under running water, then allow it to soak in a bowl of water for about 30 minutes. Drain well in a sieve. Meanwhile, put the shiitake mushrooms into a bowl with the warm water to rehydrate. After an hour, remove the mushrooms from the water, but don't discard the liquid.

2. Cut the pork into bite-sized pieces. Put into a bowl with the sake and soy sauce and allow to marinate for 15 minutes.

3. Finely slice the presoaked mushrooms. Very finely chop the garlic.

4. Put the oil into a frying pan over a medium heat, add the garlic and cook for 1 minute, taking care not to let it burn. Add the chopped pork and cook for 5–7 minutes until the edges crisp up a little.

5. When the pork is well cooked, add the mushrooms and cook for a further 2 minutes. Now set the frying pan aside.

6. Put the rice into your rice cooker. Add the soy sauce, sake, sugar, chicken stock powder, salt and five-spice powder. Pour in the remaining water from the soaked shiitake mushrooms and top up with extra water until it meets the 3-cup water level mark. Add the cooked pork and mushrooms into the rice cooker. Set the cooker according to the maker's instructions.

7. Once it's cooked, mix the sticky contents well and serve on a plate with a sprinkling of sesame seeds and chopped spring onion, if you like.

STORE-CUPBOARD CURRY

Serves 2

I call this recipe Store-cupboard Curry, as it is a great way of including whatever I happen to have left over or in need of using up, alongside those perennial ingredients such as raisins and, in this case, pistachio nuts. You can substitute ingredients as you wish, or omit those items you don't have to hand. Either way, it creates an easy, no-stress supper.

- 2 rice cooker cups Thai fragrant (jasmine) rice
- 1 tablespoon chicken stock powder
- 100 ml (3½ fl oz/scant ½ cup) warm water
- 100 grams (3½ oz) pistachios
- 35 grams (1½ oz) smoked bacon rashers (slices)
- 1 clove garlic
- 50 grams (2 oz) white onion
- 50 grams (2 oz) carrot
- 50 grams (2 oz/⅓ cup) canned sweetcorn
- 1 teaspoon olive oil
- 2 teaspoons curry powder (mild, medium or hot, depending on your preference)
- 30 grams (1 oz) raisins

1. Rinse your rice thoroughly under running water until the water runs clear, then add it to the rice cooker pot. Dissolve your chicken stock powder in the warm water to make a broth. Set it aside to cool.
2. Peel the skins from the pistachios and roughly chop the nuts. Finely chop the bacon rashers and slice the garlic finely. Very finely chop the carrots and onions. Drain the liquid from your tin of sweet corn.
3. Now add the olive oil to a frying pan over a medium heat. Once it is hot, toss in two thirds of the pistachios, the chopped bacon, carrots, onion, garlic and corn. Sprinkle over the curry powder and fry everything until the bacon is cooked and the aroma is coming out of the curry spices. Turn off the heat.
4. Pour the chicken broth over the rice in the rice cooker. Add extra water to fill the rice cooker to the 2-cup water level mark. Add the cooled, curried bacon and veg from the frying pan.
5. Set the cooker according to the maker's instructions. When the rice is cooked, toss in the raisins and mix. Serve on a plate and sprinkle with the remaining chopped pistachios to finish.

CHICKEN RICE WITH TOMATO

Serves 1

One of the cheaper cuts of chicken are the thighs. Not only are they more affordable than chicken breast, but they are often juicier, less prone to drying out and far more flavoursome. This also makes them an ideal meat choice for rice-cooker cooking, as they will happily cook among other ingredients without much need for attention or fuss.

1 rice cooker cup Thai fragrant (jasmine) rice
200 grams (7 oz/¾ cup) canned diced tomatoes
150 grams (5 oz) boneless chicken thighs
2 button (white) mushrooms
20 grams (¾ oz/1½ tablespoons) salted butter
1 chicken stock (bouillon) cube

1. Rinse your rice thoroughly under running water until the water runs clear, then add it to the rice cooker pot, followed by the canned tomatoes.

2. Cut the chicken thigh meat into bite-sized pieces and add them to the pot. Roughly slice the mushrooms and add them to the pot, too.

3. Cut the butter into small chunks and place them over the rice, chicken and mushrooms. Finally, dilute the chicken stock cube in 2 tablespoons of water and add to the pot.

4. Set the cooker according to the maker's instructions. Once it's cooked, open the lid and give the contents a stir to mix everything and it's ready to eat, piping hot.

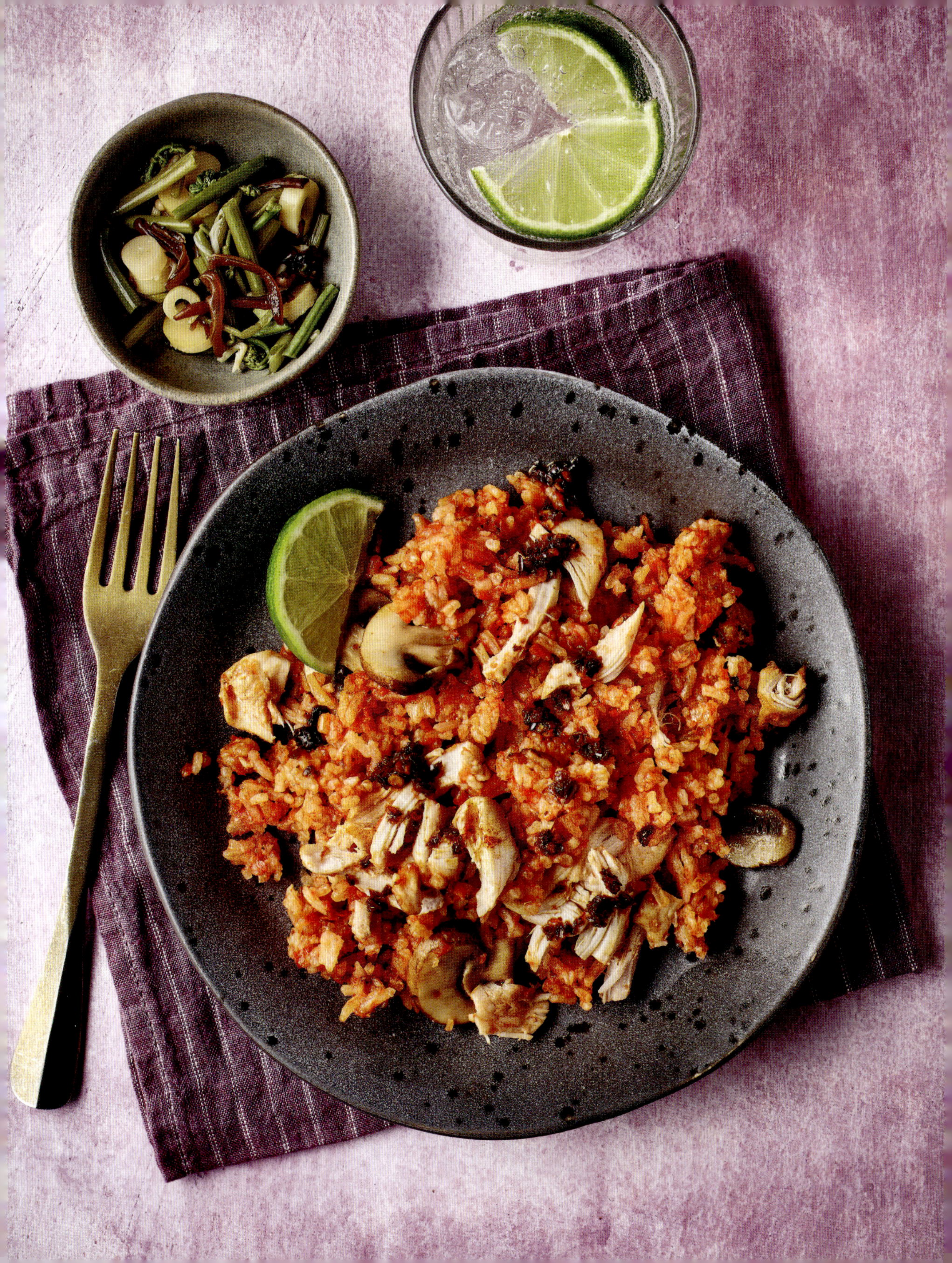

JAMBALAYA RICE

Serves 1

We tend to think of jambalaya as a dish from the southern part of the United States, in particular Louisiana, enjoyed to the sounds of creole music. However, its roots and influences are likely to have come from Africa, Spain and France. A cacophony of ingredients make this recipe a vibrant, indulgent feast in a bowl that is a perfect dish to entertain gatherings – with little preparation fuss.

1 rice cooker cup japonica rice
125 grams (4 oz) boneless chicken thigh
¼ white onion
½ green bell pepper
¼ red bell pepper
20 grams (¾ oz/2 tablespoons) canned sweetcorn
Salt and pepper, to taste
1 tablespoon olive oil
1 tablespoon cooking sake
2 tablespoons tomato ketchup
½ teaspoon Tabasco sauce
1 teaspoon curry powder (mild, medium or hot, depending on your preference)
½ teaspoon chicken stock powder
Water, as needed
Flat leaf parsley, chopped, to garnish (optional)

1. Rinse your rice under cold water in a sieve for a few minutes until the water runs clear. Tip it into a bowl and cover it with water to soak for at least 30 minutes, then drain well.
2. Meanwhile cut the onion, green pepper and red pepper into roughly 1-cm (½-inch) cubes. Drain the sweetcorn.
3. Season the chicken thigh meat with salt and pepper.
4. Put half the olive oil (1½ teaspoons) into a frying pan over a medium heat. When hot, add the chicken skin side down and cook for a few minutes until browned. Turn it over, cook for a minute or so on the other side, then remove.
5. Put the remaining olive oil (1½ teaspoons) into the same frying pan, again over a medium heat. Add the onion and fry until soft, then add the green pepper, red pepper and sweetcorn. Stir-fry for a minute or so until the oil coats all of the vegetables, then add the sake, ketchup, Tabasco, curry powder, chicken stock powder and a pinch of salt. Stir-fry for a further couple of minutes to allow the moisture to evaporate.
6. Put the soaked rice in the rice cooker pot and add enough water to just below the 1-cup water level mark. Now add the stir-fried

vegetables and flatten out the rice surface. Place the chicken thighs on top and set the cooker according to the maker's instructions.

7. Remove the chicken and mix the remaining contents together so the flavoured vegetables are evenly distributed. Cut the chicken into bite-sized pieces.
8. Scoop the rice and vegetables into a bowl and top with the chicken pieces. Sprinkle with parsley if desired.

GARLIC SAUSAGE RICE

Serves 1

Rice-cooker cooking allows all the ingredients to impart their flavours through the rice, adding extra layers of savouriness. This recipe infuses the rice with the smoky hint of frankfurters and fragrant pungency of garlic. It is a favourite with my children, both when they were younger and still now they are grown up.

1 rice cooker cup japonica rice
200 ml (7 fl oz/scant 1 cup) water
2 tablespoons Japanese soy sauce
1 skinny frankfurter sausage
6 cloves garlic
1 chicken stock (bouillon) cube
Knob (pat) of salted butter
Black pepper, to taste
Sesame seeds, to garnish

1. Rinse your rice thoroughly under running water, until the water runs clear, then add it to the rice cooker pot. Pour in the water and add the soy sauce. Swirl it lightly with a chopstick to distribute it.
2. Slice your frankfurter into 5-mm (¼-inch) thick slices and scatter them into the pot. Finely slice your garlic cloves and add them to the rice cooker pot. Finally, crumble you chicken stock cube over the rice and sausage mixture and stir it through.
3. Set the cooker according to the maker's instructions. Once it's cooked, open the lid, add the knob of butter and give the contents a stir to mix everything together.
4. Serve with a generous twist of black pepper and a scattering of sesame seeds.

SIMPLE COCONUT RICE

Serves 1

Coconut milk is an Asian culinary cornerstone and makes such a useful store-cupboard staple. It really elevates the taste of any rice dish, naturally sweetening it as well as adding fragrant, subtle nutty notes. This bowl can be eaten as is or used to up the ante as a side.

1 rice cooker cup Thai fragrant (jasmine) rice
½ teaspoon freshly grated ginger
100 ml (3½ fl oz/scant ½ cup) coconut milk
Pinch of salt
Water, as needed

1. Rinse your rice under cold water for a few minutes, until the water runs clear. Drain the rice in a sieve and allow it to sit in the sieve for about 10 minutes.

2. Meanwhile, grate a small amount of fresh ginger root. (You can use powder at a pinch.)

3. Now place the rice in the rice cooker and pour in the coconut milk, then add the grated ginger and a pinch of salt.

4. Fill the rice cooker pot to the 1-cup water level mark and set the cooker according to the maker's instructions. Once cooked, open the rice cooker lid and stir the contents. Serve with the accompaniment of your choice.

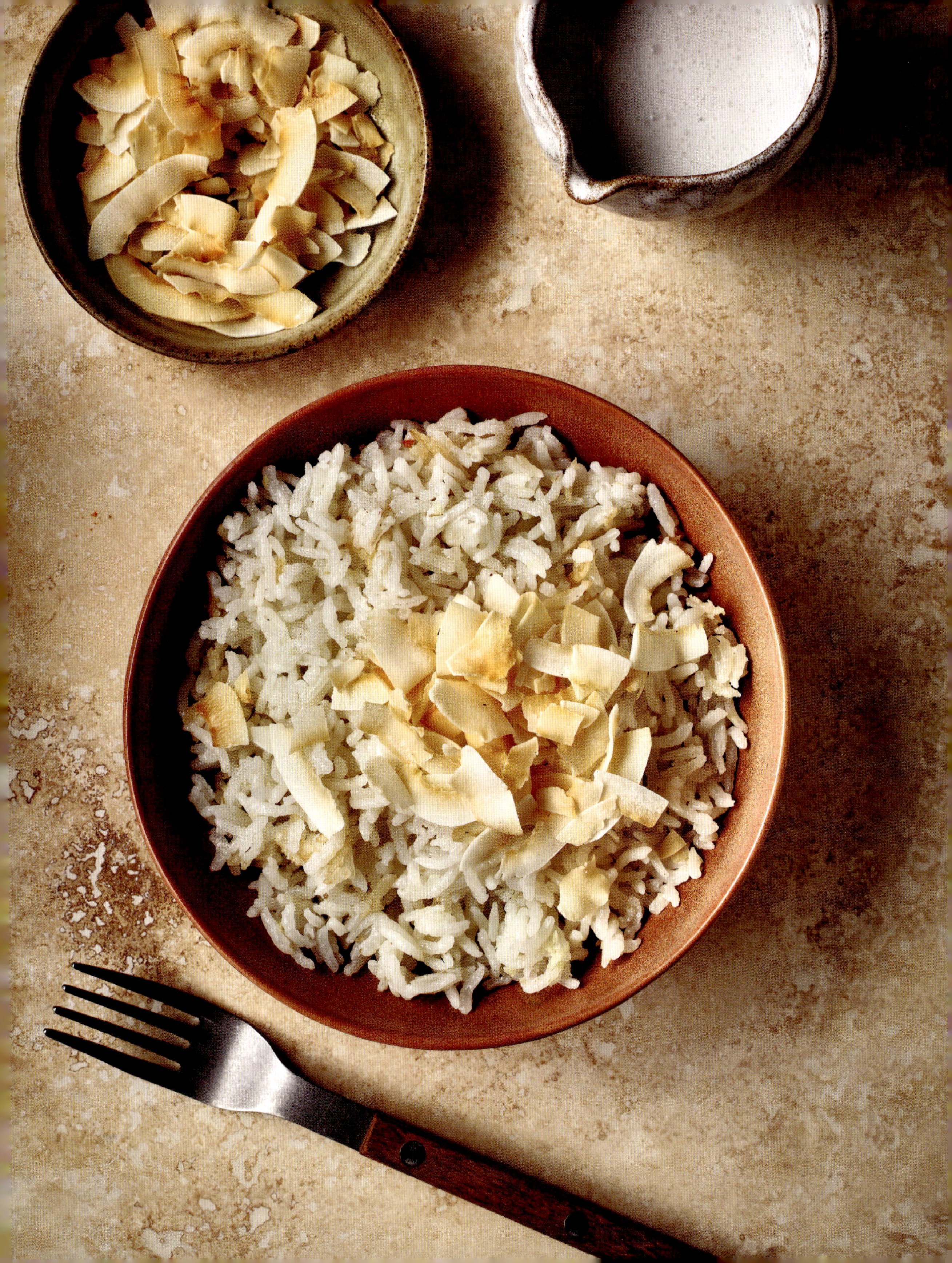

BUTTERED SARDINE RICE

Serves 2

Canned sardines are bursting with omega fats that are great for your health. But we often need inspiration on how to combine them in a dish. This recipe takes the simple fish and gives it a Japanese umami twist by including shiitake mushrooms and a dashi stock.

2 rice cooker cups Thai fragrant (jasmine) rice
100 grams (3½ oz) shiitake mushrooms
Water, as needed
2 tablespoons white dashi stock
150 grams (5 oz) canned sardines in oil
20 grams (¾ oz/1½ tablespoons) salted butter
2–3 spring onions (scallions), finely chopped

1. Rinse your rice under cold water in a sieve for a few minutes, until the water runs clear. Tip it into a bowl and cover with water to soak for at least 30 minutes, then drain well. Meanwhile, cut off the stalks from the shiitake mushrooms and break them up.

2. Now put the drained rice in the rice cooker pot and add water up to the 2-cup water level mark.

3. Add the white dashi stock and the canned sardines with their juices, breaking them up a little. Place the lid on and set the cooker according to the maker's instructions. Once the rice is done cooking, add the salted butter and mix well with a rice spoon until the flavours are well blended.

4. Spoon into serving bowls, sprinkle with the chopped spring onions, and it's done.

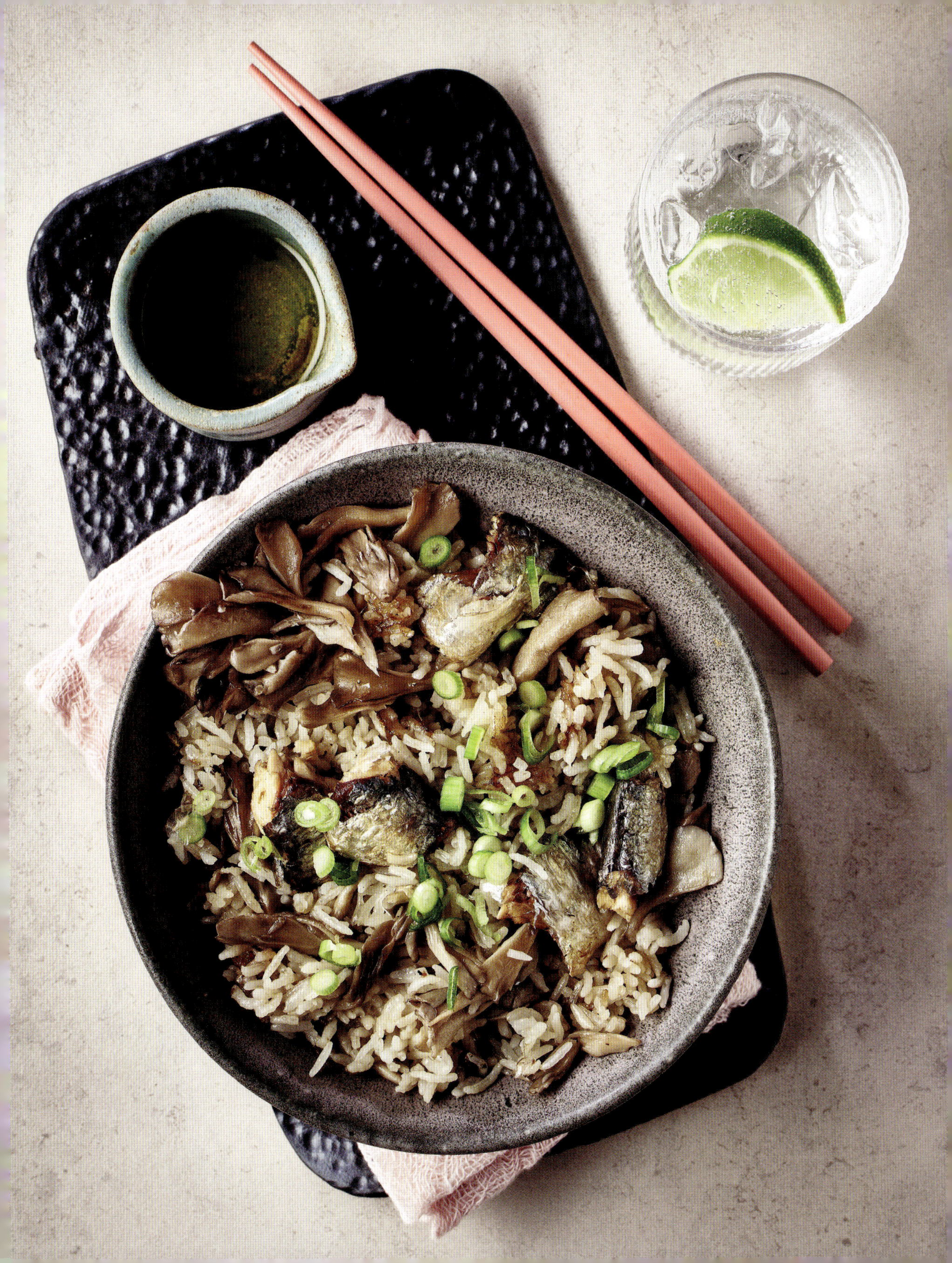

SHREDDED CHICKEN & SPRING ONION RICE

Serves 2

Shredded or pulled cooked meats often require long, slow cooking times. By using the steam of a rice cooker, the meat softens more readily, allowing you to shred and enjoy the broken-up texture, combined with the flavour-infused rice.

---

2 rice cooker cups Thai fragrant (jasmine) rice
2 boneless, skin-on chicken thighs
1 thumb-sized piece fresh root ginger
2 tablespoons cooking sake
1 teaspoon chicken stock powder
½ teaspoon salt
Pepper, to taste
Water, as needed

Spring onion dressing
165 grams (6 oz/10–12 medium) spring onions (scallions)
½ teaspoon salt
Pepper, to taste
1 tablespoon sesame oil
1 tablespoon lemon juice

1. Rinse your rice under cold water in a sieve for a few minutes, until the water runs clear. Tip it into a bowl and cover with water to soak it for at least 30 minutes, then drain well.

2. Meanwhile, trim any excess fat from the chicken but leave the skin on for now, as it adds flavour to the dish. Slice the ginger into thin batons.

3. Now put the soaked rice, cooking sake, chicken stock powder, salt and pepper into the rice cooker pot. Fill the pot with water up to the 2-cup water level mark.

4. Mix everything together and flatten the rice so it will cook evenly. Place the ginger slices and chicken thighs on top, skin side down, and set the cooker according to the maker's instructions.

5. As it cooks, finely chop the spring onions and put them into a small bowl. Add the salt, pepper, sesame oil and lemon juice to the bowl and mix well.

6. Once the rice cooker is ready, open the lid and remove the ginger and chicken. Pull the chicken flesh into bite-sized pieces, remove the skin, add it back to the rice and mix well.

7. Place the flavoured rice in two bowls and pour over the salty, spring onion dressing.

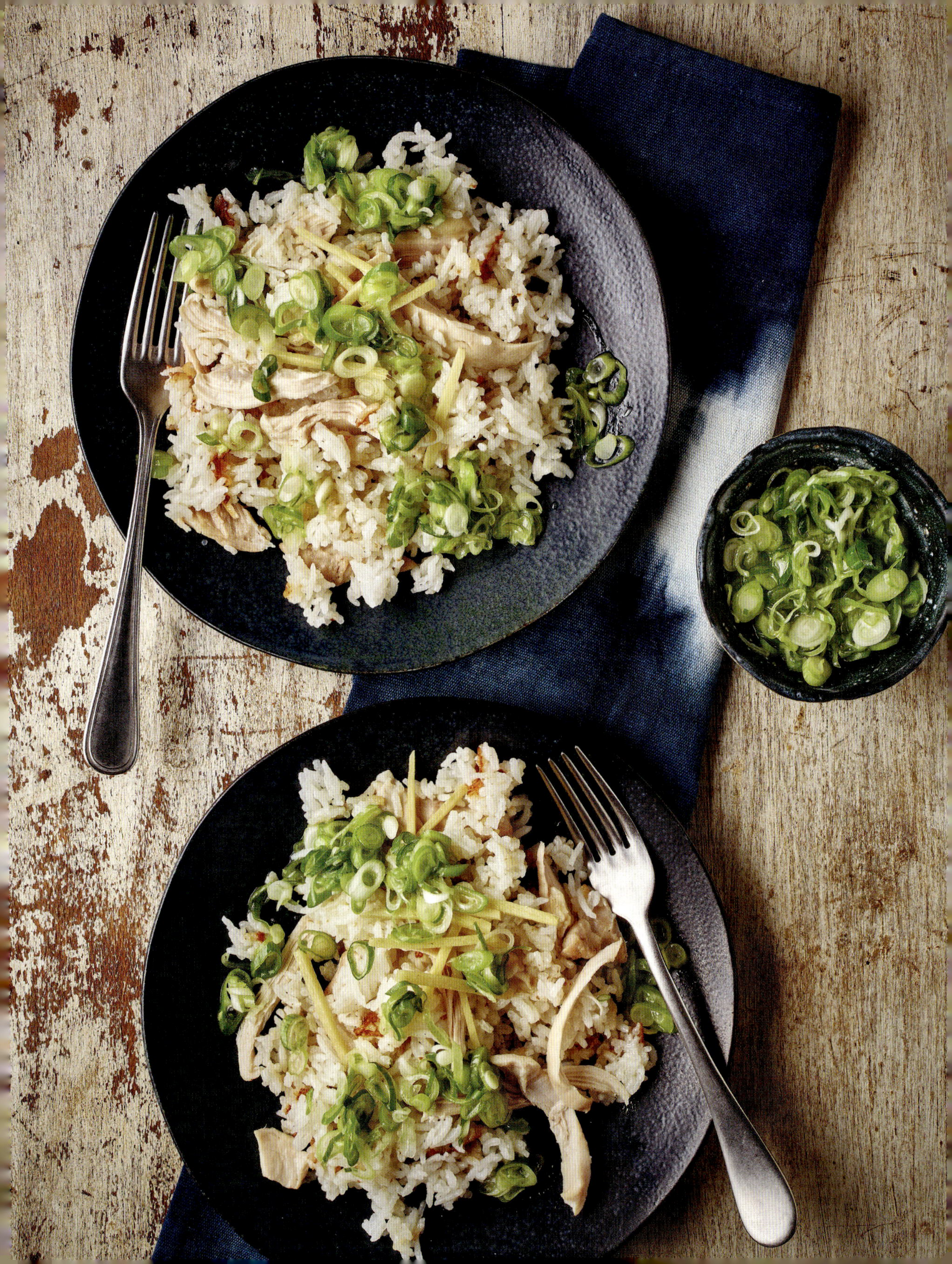

CHESTNUT RICE

Serves 2

Although chestnuts are often associated with autumn, you can find cooked whole chestnuts in the supermarket all year round. The combination of the slightly sweet, chestnut flesh melds beautifully with the saltiness of the rice. Try this rice dish as a meat-free alternative, filled with the protein, vitamins and minerals from these delightful nuts.

---

2 rice cooker cups japonica rice
250 grams (8½ oz/2 cups) peeled, cooked, chestnuts
2 tablespoons cooking sake
½ teaspoon salt
½ teaspoon chicken stock powder
Water, as needed
Black sesame seeds, to garnish

See the chapter opener for this recipe's image.

1. Rinse your rice under cold water in a sieve for a few minutes, until the water runs clear. Tip it into a bowl and cover it with water to soak it for at least 30 minutes, then drain well.

2. Remove the chestnuts from the jar or packaging and drain or pat away any excess water. Put the rice, sake and salt into the pot of the rice cooker, then sprinkle over the chicken stock powder. Add water up to the 2-cup water level mark and mix everything gently. Add the whole chestnuts and set the cooker according to the maker's instructions.

3. Transfer to two bowls and sprinkle with black sesame seeds.

SEAFOOD RICE

Serves 2

Seafood dishes often seem time-sensitive, with fish being one of those ingredients we tend to watch over closely because it cooks to the minute. That's not the case here: the beauty of this rice-cooker recipe is everything will stay moist and tender, and will be cooked to perfection without the need to fuss over it. And, the rice soaks up the delicious seafood liquor as it cooks, adding extra flavour.

---

2 rice cooker cups japonica rice
150 grams (5 oz) frozen mixed seafood
½ white onion
½ green bell pepper
50 grams (2 oz/⅓ cup) canned sweetcorn
½ teaspoon chicken stock powder
scant ¾ teaspoon salt
Black pepper, to taste
Water, as needed
1 tablespoon salted butter
Chives or coriander (cilantro), chopped (optional)

1. Rinse the rice under cold water in a sieve for a few minutes, until the water runs clear. Tip it into a bowl and cover with water to soak for at least 30 minutes, then drain well.

2. Meanwhile, get on with the ingredient prep. Thaw your frozen seafood mix. You can do this in a bowl of cold water, but rinse well afterwards.

3. Now, finely chop the onion, and cut the pepper in half and deseed it before chopping it into small cubes. Drain the canned sweetcorn.

4. Put the rice, chicken stock powder, salt and pepper into the rice cooker pot. Now add water to the cooker pot up to just below the 2-cup water level mark. Mix everything together and flatten the rice so it all cooks evenly. Spread the chopped onion, green pepper, sweetcorn and seafood mix on top of the rice and top with a little butter cut into small pieces. Now set the cooker according to the maker's instructions.

5. Once cooked, stir well from the bottom so everything is mixed together and serve on two plates.

6. Sprinkle with chopped chives or coriander if you wish.

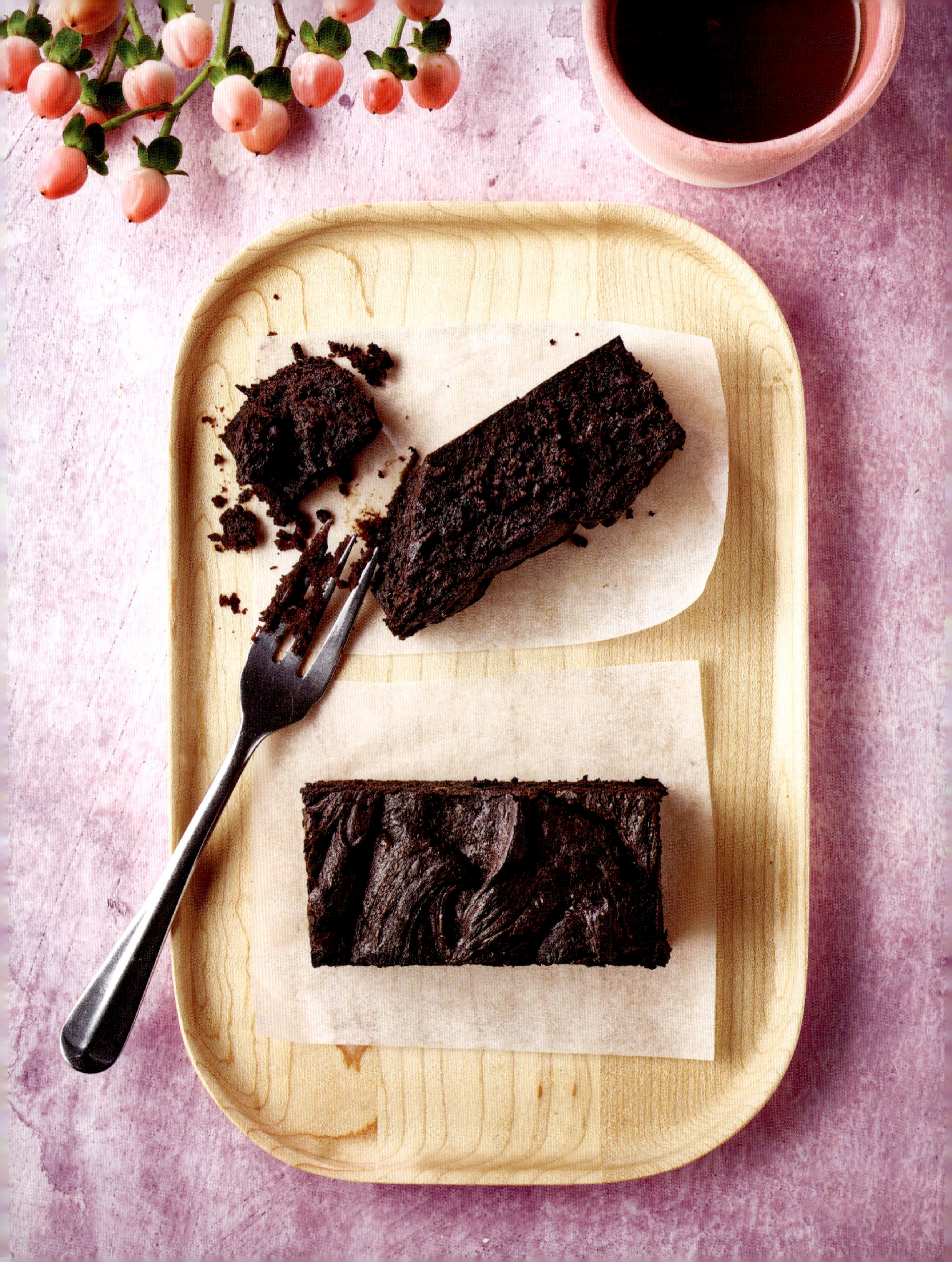

RICE FLOUR

Rice flour is made from finely milled, raw rice grains. It is a staple ingredient in Chinese, Japanese, Thai, Korean and other Asian cultures. It is gluten-free, making it a superb choice for those following a gluten-free diet (such as people who have coeliac disease), who still want to experience baked treats and the like. Even sticky (glutinous) rice is free from gluten. The name refers to the sticky texture due to its starch content. Brown rice flour varieties are high in insoluble fibre, making them a great digestive cleanser, and have a high protein content and a healthy helping of the B vitamins. And when you are done with the delicious savoury pancakes, muffins and sweet treat *mochi* in this chapter, you can also use rice flour in your skincare regime.

FLUFFY RICE FLOUR PANCAKES

Serves 2

These pancakes are egg-free, making them a super-speedy breakfast option that uses only store-cupboard (pantry) ingredients. If you do wish to create a classic Japanese souffle pancake, then simply add in a whisked egg white to the batter mix and watch them rise. Japanese pancakes are often served with savoury accompaniments such as *okonomiyaki* sauce, which is similar to Worcestershire sauce, creamy Japanese mayonnaise, *katsuoboshi* (shaved bonito flakes) and *aonori*, a powdered green seaweed.

---

150 grams (5 oz/1 cup) Asian rice flour
5 grams (¼ oz/1 teaspoon) baking powder
200 ml (7 fl oz/scant 1 cup) milk
2 tablespoons sugar
1 tablespoon light sesame oil or olive oil
Topping of your choice

1. For making pancakes, there is no need to sieve (sift) the rice flour first.
2. In a large bowl, mix the rice flour and baking powder together thoroughly. Add the milk, sugar, and light sesame oil (or olive oil) and mix the batter well until there are no lumps.
3. Now, put a lidded frying pan over high heat until hot, then reduce the heat to low. I use a non-stick frying pan, so there is no need to add additional oil into the pan as the mixture won't stick.
4. Spoon one quarter of the batter mix onto the hot frying pan to form a roughly 6-cm (2½-inch) diameter pancake. Allow it to cook for about 1 minute until bubbles appear. Don't move it about and don't cover the frying pan yet.

5. Once it is golden brown on the underside, flip the pancake over and cover the pan with the lid. Continue to cook over a low heat for a further 2–3 minutes, then remove. Repeat this process until all of your batter is used up.
6. Enjoy your pancakes. Top with maple syrup and blueberries or any other topping of your choice.

RICE FLOUR PIZZA

Serves 2

The gluten-free attributes of rice flour make it an ideal ingredient when enjoying pizza baking at home. You can find white and brown varieties that offer even more beneficial fibre. It's easy to work with, and the results are well worth sampling. This recipe is laden with salty pepperoni and colourful vegetables, but once you have mastered the base, you can be as creative as you like with the toppings.

For the base
150 grams (5 oz/1 cup) rice flour, plus extra for dusting
1 teaspoon baking powder
1½ teaspoons sugar
Pinch of salt
1 tablespoon olive oil
100 ml (3½ fl oz/scant ½ cup) warm water

Pizza toppings
¼ medium white onion
30 grams (1 oz/¼ medium) green bell pepper
4 cherry tomatoes
3 tablespoons pizza sauce
4 slices (80 grams/3 oz) pepperoni
40 grams (1½ oz/⅓ cup) grated pizza cheese, such as mozzarella

1. Preheat the oven to 180°C (350°F).
2. Thinly slice the onion. Cut the stalk off the bell pepper and remove the seeds, then slice the amount you need into roughly 3-mm (⅛-inch) thick rings. Remove any stalks from the cherry tomatoes and slice them into halves.
3. To make the pizza base (crust), mix the rice flour, baking powder, sugar and salt in a bowl. Add the olive oil and lukewarm water and mix until the flour is no longer lumpy, then bring it all together to form a dough.
4. Spread out a sheet of baking (parchment) paper and lift the dough out of the bowl (add a little flour to your fingers so it doesn't stick). Cover the dough with more baking paper and, using a rolling pin, gently roll out into a circle about 25 cm (10 inches) in diameter.
5. Peel off the baking paper covering the dough and lift the bottom sheet with the dough on it onto a baking sheet.

6. Spread the pizza sauce evenly over the base and then place the onion slices, green pepper slices, pepperoni slices and lastly, the cherry tomato halves over it. Top with the pizza cheese, sprinkling it evenly over the pizza.
7. Bake in the preheated oven for about 15 minutes. Slice and serve.

RICE FLOUR TEMPURA

Serves 2

When the Portuguese arrived in Japan centuries ago, they brought with them a love of deep-fried, flour-coated foods. The Japanese subsequently made it their own, and the tempura light thin batter is a traditional national dish. Incorporating rice flour is a variation on the classic batter, making the air-light crunch of crispy tempura even more delicate. For an exceptional tempura batter to coat your favourite vegetables and seafood, make sure the water you use is extra chilled.

- 100 grams (3½ oz/⅔ cup) rice flour, plus extra for dusting
- 1 teaspoon Japanese soy sauce
- 200 ml (7 fl oz/scant 1 cup) chilled sparkling water
- 1 large (US extra-large) egg
- Tempura filling ingredients of your choice: vegetable strips (e.g. carrot, bell pepper, courgette/zucchini), rounds (e.g. aubergine/eggplant) or seafood (e.g. prawns/shrimp)
- Vegetable oil, for deep-frying
- Tempura dipping sauce (see box opposite), to serve

1. Combine the rice flour, soy sauce and chilled sparkling water in a bowl, then crack in the egg and mix well using a whisk to create an aerated batter. The batter should be thick enough to drip continuously off a metal spoon.

2. Prepare your favourite tempura ingredients, and be sure to pat them dry with kitchen paper towels to wipe off any excess water.

3. Add enough vegetable oil to a high-sided frying pan to fill it to a depth of 3 cm (1¼ inches), and place it over high heat until it reaches 180°C (350°F).

4. Now dip the ingredients into the batter; as rice flour tends to settle, stir it each time before dipping in the ingredients. Working with one piece at a time, dip into the batter, ensuring an even coating.

5. Carefully lower the batter-coated ingredient into the hot oil and fry it until it is a light golden brown and floats to the surface. Remove from the oil with a slotted spoon and drain away any excess oil on a piece of kitchen paper towel before serving.
6. Serve with the tempura dipping sauce.

TEMPURA DIPPING SAUCE

150 ml (5 fl oz/⅔ cup) water
5 grams (¼ oz/scant ½ cup) bonito flakes
2 tablespoons mirin
2 tablespoons Japanese soy sauce
1 tablespoon sugar

Put the water in a saucepan over a medium heat and add the bonito flakes. Simmer for 3–4 minutes. Scoop out the bonito flakes. Now add the mirin, soy sauce and sugar, and simmer for a further 3–4 minutes until the sugar dissolves.

RICE FLOUR

RICE FLOUR GYOZA

Makes 10–12 pieces

Gyoza are a specific type of dumpling that are always crescent-shaped in form. Closely related to Chinese *jiaozi*, the gyoza contain sumptuous fillings (often minced pork, chicken or prawn/shrimp) wrapped in a beautifully semi-chewy, nearly translucent dough. This recipe provides you with everything you need to start preparing your own gyoza. If you want to make a batch to use at another date, they are perfect for freezing, to store for whenever you are in the mood for homemade dumplings. Simply sprinkle with a little flour before freezing to keep the wrappers separated.

Filling
80 grams (3 oz) minced (ground) pork or chicken
1 teaspoon Japanese soy sauce
1 teaspoon sesame oil
½ teaspoon salt
1 teaspoon cooking sake or white wine
1 clove garlic, grated
2 teaspoons cornflour (cornstarch)
100 grams (3½ oz/1½ cups prepared) Chinese (napa) cabbage, finely sliced

1. For the filling: put the mince, soy sauce, sesame oil, salt, sake, garlic and cornflour in a bowl and mix well. Slice the cabbage into tiny pieces and add. Work the mixture together and set aside.

2. For the dough wrappers: mix cornflour and water in a small saucepan, put it over a gentle heat and heat until it becomes translucent, has thickened and no longer changes consistency.

3. Add the rice flour to a bowl, then pour in the cornflour mixture and add a pinch of salt while it's still hot. Blend them together and knead. Be careful not to burn yourself on the hot cornflour.

4. When it starts to come together, add the oil and knead some more. The dough will become a little sticky – when it does, dust with a little extra rice flour so you can pick it up without getting messy.

Wrappers, makes 10–12 6 5-cm (2-inch) diameter wrappers
20 grams (1 oz) cornflour (cornstarch) or tapioca flour
120 ml (4 fl oz/½ cup) water
100 grams (3 oz/⅔ cup) rice flour, plus extra for dusting
Pinch of salt
1 teaspoon olive oil
Drizzle of vegetable oil, for frying
3 tablespoons water

5. Place the dough on a board sprinkled with a little more rice flour, then roll it out with a rolling pin to about the same thickness as a cooked lasagne sheet. It dries out easily, so cover it with cling film (plastic wrap) while forming the gyozas.

6. Using a 5-cm (2-inch) diameter cutter, stamp out a gyoza wrapper (cover the dough again), then place a little of the filling mixture on one half of the wrapper, fold over and pinch the edges together to seal. Repeat with the remaining dough and filling.

7. Heat a frying pan with a little vegetable oil, place each gyoza in the pan and cook until the bottoms are golden, turning them over to colour the other side. Then add the water, put a lid over the pan and simmer for 3–4 minutes until the water has evaporated.

RICE FLOUR

CHEESY RICE FLOUR MUFFINS

Makes 4–5 muffins
You will need six 7x4.5-cm (2.75x1.75-inch) silicone muffin moulds

The Japanese will happily add sugar to rice-flour dishes to enhance their flavour. Cream cheese is a very popular dairy ingredient in Japan, and it enhances the creaminess of baked goods, such as in this slightly sweetened, savoury snack. This recipe requires the muffin batter to be steamed, not baked. These muffins are delicious – both fluffy and chewy – and can be enjoyed straight from the pan.

140 ml (5 fl oz/scant ⅔ cup) milk
40 grams (1½ oz/3 tablespoons) cream cheese
4 slices Cheddar cheese
2 medium (US large) eggs
70 grams (2½ oz/6 tablespoons) sugar
40 grams (1½ oz/3 tablespoons) rice bran oil
160 grams (5½ oz/1 cup) rice flour
2 teaspoons baking powder
Large drizzle of vegetable oil

1. Combine the milk, cream cheese and sliced cheese in a saucepan over a low heat, and heat until all of the cheese has melted into a sauce. The smoother the sauce, the smoother the batter will be. Once melted, turn off the heat and wait until cooled.

2. Put the eggs and sugar into a bowl and beat well with a whisk. Now add the egg mixture to the cheese sauce, little by little, while mixing thoroughly with the whisk. Add in the rice bran oil and again mix thoroughly.

3. Tip in the rice flour and baking powder and mix.

4. Divide the mixture among individual muffin moulds. Place the moulds into a steamer pan or basket over a saucepan of simmering water, then steam for about 15 minutes. The muffins are ready when a skewer (or toothpick) comes out clean when inserted into the centre of a muffin.

5. Remove the muffins from the moulds. Wipe the bottom of a frying pan with a little vegetable oil, place it over a medium heat. When hot, add the muffins topside down and fry until the tops are golden brown.
6. Enjoy the muffins hot right after steaming or, after they have cooled, wrap the muffins in cling film (plastic wrap) to store.

RICE FLOUR

RICE FLOUR AND YOGURT NAAN BREAD

Makes 3

Despite what you might think, the Japanese are very keen on bread. The renowned, fluffy Japanese milk bread is a favourite and is often eaten alongside breakfast plates. Its soft, cloud-like texture adds another dimension. It is also used to make pillowy sandwiches. *Sozai pan* is a savoury-filled bready snack and closer to the stuffed naan breads of Indian cookery. This recipe is the perfect gluten-free alternative for those who love the comfort of a bread-based side dish with a hint of cheesiness.

---

150 grams (5 oz/1 cup) rice flour, plus extra for dusting
90 grams (3 oz/⅓ cup) natural (plain) yogurt
1 tablespoon white sugar
3 tablespoons milk
5 grams (scant ¼ oz/1 teaspoon) baking powder
Pinch of salt
1 teaspoon olive oil
Handful of grated Cheddar cheese

1. Put the rice flour, plain yogurt, sugar, milk, baking powder and salt into a bowl and combine well using a rubber spatula. Once combined, knead the mixture in the bowl until it forms a doughy ball.

2. Rub your hands with a little olive oil to prevent the dough sticking, and then divide the dough ball into roughly three parts. Place each piece of dough on a floured board or work surface and sprinkle a little grated cheese over each. Now roll out the dough thinly to 3-4 mm (¼ inch) thick.

3. Carefully transfer each piece to a non-stick frying pan over a medium heat and cook for around 2 minutes on each side. Once slightly puffed up and golden in places, it is ready to serve and enjoy, dipped in a fragrant soup or with a Japanese curry.

RICE FLOUR BROWNIES

Makes 2–3

Enjoy a treat for one with this quick and easy brownie recipe. A hint of rum and the rich bitterness of dark chocolate make this version a little more on the grown-up side. If you want to make larger batches, simply double or triple the ingredient quantities as required.

---

100 grams (3½ oz) dark chocolate
30 grams (1 oz/2 tablespoons) coconut oil
1 tablespoon single (light) cream
30 grams (1 oz/3 tablespoons) rice flour
10 grams (scant ½ oz/2 tablespoons) unsweetened cocoa powder
1½ teaspoons rum (optional)
1 medium (US large) egg
20 grams (¾ oz/1½ tablespoons) sugar
30 grams (1 oz/3 tablespoons) chocolate chips

See the chapter opener for this recipe's image.

1. Preheat the oven to 170°C (340°F).
2. Put the chocolate and coconut oil into a glass bowl and melt slowly over a saucepan of simmering water. Add the cream, rice flour, cocoa powder and rum and mix.
3. Crack the egg into another bowl and add the sugar, then mix well with a whisk. Once mixed, add it to the chocolate mixture and mix well with a whisk. Once thoroughly mixed, toss in the chocolate chips and mix in using a spatula.
4. Pour the mixture gently into a greased and floured small tray and bake in the preheat oven for about 17 minutes.
5. Once cooled, remove the brownie cake from the tray and cut into pieces, ready to serve.

STRAWBERRIES & CREAM MOCHI

Makes 8

Authentic soft, squishy mochi are a sensorial treat. I make this recipe with my mochi students, and it is always received really well. Fun and delicious, be sure to make extra, as they have a tendency to disappear fast!

- 100 grams (3½ oz/⅔ cup) sticky (glutinous) rice flour, plus extra for dusting
- 30 grams (1 oz/¼ cup) cornflour (cornstarch)
- 50 grams (2 oz/⅓ cup) fresh strawberries, rinsed, stalks removed
- 120 ml (4 fl oz/½ cup) milk (I use oat milk)
- 40 grams (1½ oz/scant ¼ cup) sugar
- 30 grams (1 oz/2 tablespoons) salted butter, cut into small pieces
- 150 grams (5 oz/½ cup) azuki bean paste
- 40 ml (1½ fl oz/scant 3 tablespoons) double (heavy) cream, whipped

1. Put the rice flour and cornflour into a microwave-safe container. Set aside. Choose a few strawberries for the filling and set them aside.

2. Now put the remaining strawberries, the milk and the sugar into a blender. Blend until thoroughly smooth. Pour the strawberry milk into the microwave-safe container with the flour mixture and stir until the mixture has a yogurt-like texture. Cover the container with microwave-safe cling film (plastic wrap) and with a cocktail stick (toothpick), poke about 16 holes through the film.

3. Microwave (800W) for 3 minutes. Remove and check the texture by poking a cocktail stick into the mochi dough mixture. If the tip of the cocktail stick comes out dry, the mochi dough is fully cooked. If the tip comes out wet, place the cling film back over the container and microwave for a further 30 seconds.

4. Take the mochi out of the microwave, and put knobs of butter on top. The heat of the mochi dough will melt the butter. Put on non-stick, food-handling gloves, or rub some melted butter

on your hands to prevent them getting sticky; when the mochi dough has cooled down enough to touch, knead the dough until all the butter has been absorbed.

5. Once there's no butter left in the container, keep kneading the dough for about 5 minutes until you can pull it into a length at least 25 cm (10 inches). Transfer the mochi dough to a non-stick silicone mat, or a working surface floured with the rice flour. Apply some rice flour on the surface of the mochi dough to prevent it sticking. Cut the mochi dough with a sharp knife into 8 equal portions. With your hands or a rolling pin (covered with cling film to prevent sticking), flatten the mochi doughs into 10-cm (4-inch) diameter circles.

6. Mix the azuki bean paste with 1 tablespoon of the whipped cream.

7. Put a mochi wrapper on a soup ladle or other small round-shaped bowl to make a curved disc shape. Add some azuki filling along with half a fresh strawberry to the middle of the mochi wrapper. Pull the edges of the wrap together to cover the filling and press them together to seal well.

8. Pop the finished mochi into the freezer for 20 minutes for the best texture – and enjoy!

RICE FLOUR

RICE FLOUR CHOCOLATE CHIP COOKIES

Makes 8–10

Who doesn't love the indulgence of freshly baked chocolate chip cookies with the melting ooze of chocolate when eaten still warm. For those looking to bake gluten-free, this is the perfect recipe as it utilizes rice flour instead of wheat flour. For the best results, start making these cookies the day before – but if you can't wait, follow the shortcut!

---

50 grams (2 oz/4 tablespoons) unsalted butter, at room temperature
30 grams (1 oz/2½ tablespoons) sugar
Pinch of salt
1 egg yolk
100 grams (3½ oz/⅔ cup) rice flour
30 grams (1 oz/3 tablespoons) chocolate chips

1. The day before, put the soft butter into a mixing bowl and cream it with the flat side of a rubber spatula. Add the sugar and salt to the butter and mix well, then add the egg yolk and continue mixing until everything is well combined. Add the rice flour and mix again until the flour and butter mixture are also well combined. It will look crumbly when ready.

2. Knead the crumbly dough with your knuckles until it comes together and forms a cohesive dough. Once your doughy mixture is ready, sprinkle in the chocolate chips and knead the dough once more.

3. Divide the dough into two and shape each piece into a log. Wrap each log in cling film (plastic wrap).

4. Ideally, pop the wrapped dough logs into the fridge overnight. Alternatively, put them into the freezer for about 40 minutes. Put the baking sheet into the fridge, too, so it is also chilled.

5. Preheat the oven to 170°C (340°F). Once chilled, take out the dough and cut it into discs about 8-mm to 1-cm (½-inch) wide.
6. If the cookies have lost their shape, use your fingers to press them back into rough round shapes. Place the discs on a baking tray.
7. Pop them straight from chilled into the preheated oven and bake for 18–20 minutes. Enjoy the cookies while still warm with gooey chocolate chips!

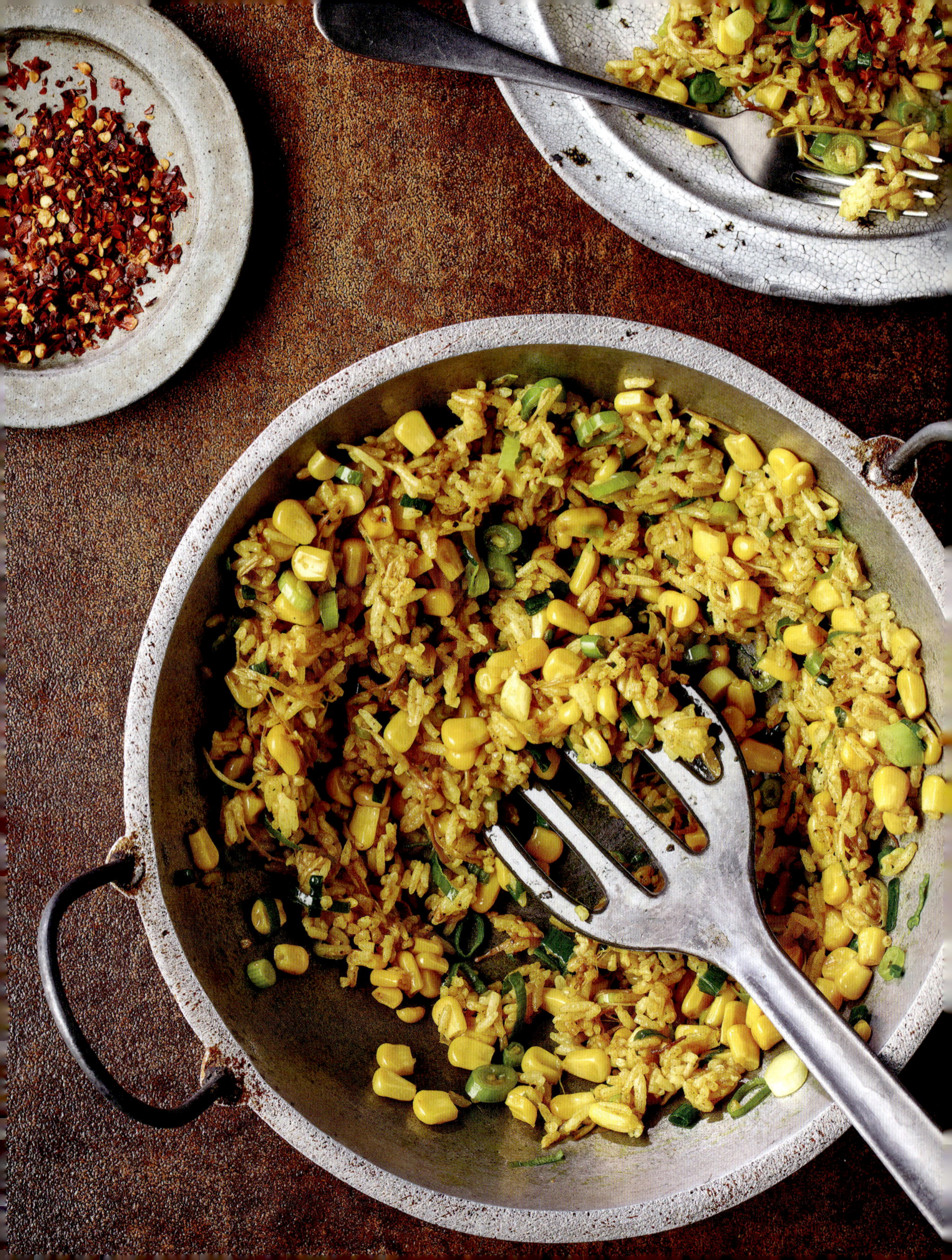

FRIED RICE

Chinese fried rice was originally conceived as a way of using up leftovers. Today, our no-waste consciences make this dish the perfect option for using up leftovers in the fridge. Of course, if you are using leftover rice, be sure to follow safe storage instructions (see page 16). Traditionally, lard would be used to add an extra unctuous sheen to the rice, but more often these days, butter is added for an additional layer of comfort. Once you have the basic cooking technique down, you can create your own signature versions of fried rice. Technique is important when making fried rice. Judging the pan's temperature and moving the ingredients around speedily will produce perfect plates, every time.

AVOCADO FRIED RICE

Serves 2

Known as "butter fruit" in China, the avocado's meteoric rise is as prevalent in Asian countries as it is in the sunny Californian Hills or the trendy eateries of London, with imports of the fruit growing by hundreds of percent. Cooked avocado may not be something you have explored before, but it is well worth sampling. In this stir-fried rice recipe, it adds a signature buttery-soft texture and a delicate flavour to this aromatic dish.

---

300 grams (10½ oz/1½ cups) cooked Thai fragrant (jasmine) rice
1 avocado
3 chipolata sausages
2 tablespoons olive oil
Pinch of salt and pepper
2 teaspoons Japanese soy sauce
½ teaspoon yuzu pepper
4 grams (⅛ oz/⅓ cup) bonito flakes

1. If you don't have leftover rice, after cooking the rice following the packet instructions, set the pan aside. Once the rice is ready, start preparing your additional ingredients. Dice the avocado and cut the sausages into 1-cm (½-inch) pieces.

2. Heat the olive oil in a high-sided frying pan or wok over a high heat, and once it is really hot, add the diced avocado and sausages. Fry quicky, until the sausages are browned.

3. Tip the cooked white rice into the pan and sprinkle over a little salt, pepper and the bonito flakes. Stir-fry over a high heat while loosening the rice and separating it, so everything is evenly distributed.

4. Pour your soy sauce into a small bowl and add the yuzu pepper, stirring until it has dissolved.

5. Make a small well in the centre of the fried rice and pour the soy sauce into the well, then combine it with the rest of the rice mixture by stirring quickly. This keeps everything crisp and not claggy.

6. After a minute, divide the mixture between two serving bowls.

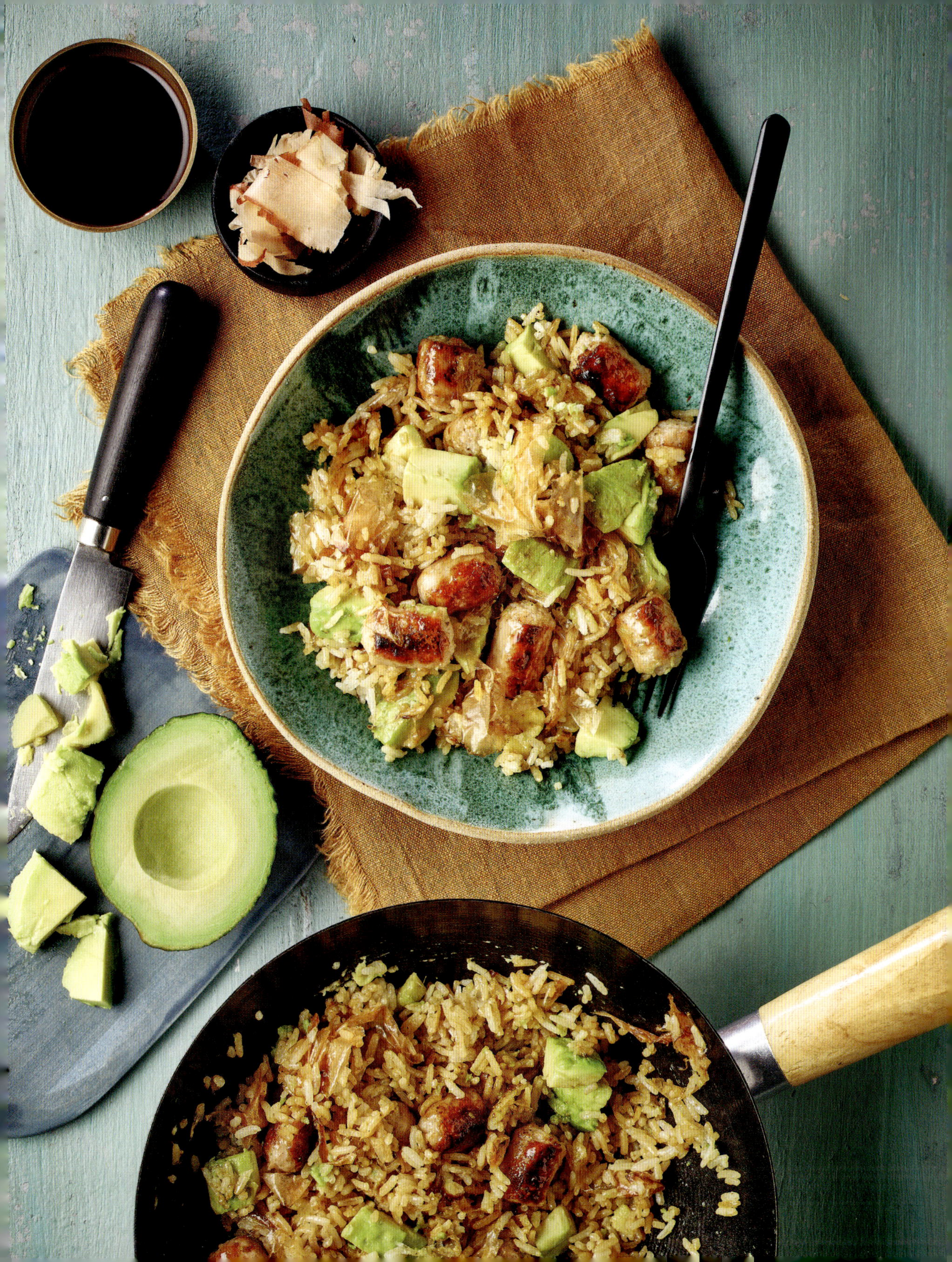

CORN CURRY FRIED RICE

Serves 2

This fried rice has the crunchy texture of the corn and the mild flavour of the enoki mushrooms. Enoki mushrooms are a favourite in Japanese cooking, not only because of their delicate stalks – they are often referred to as "skinny mushrooms" or "velvet shank" – and pale colour, but their crisp texture makes them a great choice for stir-frying as they remain firm and don't release too much water (unlike their flatter, woodier counterparts). The combination of the curry powder and butter brings out the aroma even more.

300 grams (10½ oz/1½ cups) cooked Thai fragrant (jasmine) rice
60 grams (2 oz/⅓ cup) canned sweetcorn
1 spring onion (scallion)
1 tablespoon olive oil
100 grams (3½ oz) enoki mushrooms
30 grams (1 oz/2 tablespoons) salted butter
1 tablespoon curry powder
1 tablespoon Japanese soy sauce
Salt and pepper, to taste
Chilli flakes or freshly chopped herbs, to garnish (optional)

See the chapter opener for this recipe's image.

1. If you don't have leftover rice, after cooking the rice following the packet instructions, set the pan aside. Once the rice is ready, start preparing your additional ingredients. Finely chop the spring onion and separate and slice the enoki mushroom stalks into short pieces.

2. Heat the olive oil in a high-sided frying pan or wok over a medium heat, and once it is really hot, add the corn, enoki mushrooms and spring onion and stir-fry until they change colour.

3. Add the cooked rice, breaking it up as you stir-fry, ensuring the grains are coated in the oil. Continue to stir-fry over a medium heat until the rice grains are crumbly and fully separated.

4. Add the butter, curry powder and soy sauce, and season with salt and pepper; stir-fry until everything is well combined.

5. After a minute, serve the rice piping hot into two bowls. You can add extra soy sauce, or garnish with chilli flakes or even more spring onion or fresh herbs if you wish.

FRIED RICE

CLASSIC CHINESE FRIED RICE

Serves 1

When it first appeared in China, one of the most appealing things about this one-wok meal was the economical nature of the dish. Multiple varieties sprang up, influenced by what people had to hand, what was in season and what spices they favoured. Classic Chinese fried rice has a place in many people's hearts, and the ability to produce the dish yourself at home will make this a go-to time and time again, without needing to pick up the phone to order in.

---

200 grams (7 oz/1 cup) cooked Thai fragrant (jasmine) rice
1 spring onion (scallion), chopped, plus extra finely chopped to garnish
1 medium (US large) egg
1 tablespoon sesame oil
1 teaspoon Japanese soy sauce
½ teaspoon chicken stock powder
2 pinches each of salt and pepper

1. If you don't have leftover rice, after cooking the rice following the packet instructions, set the pan aside. Once the rice is ready, start preparing your additional ingredients. Finely chop the spring onion. Crack the egg into a small bowl and beat until the yolk and white are thoroughly combined.

2. Put the sesame oil into a high-sided frying pan or wok over a medium heat. Once it is very hot, add the spring onion and stir-fry for a minute or so. Once softened, add the beaten egg and continue to stir-fry for a further minute.

3. When the egg is cooked through, tip in the cooked rice and stir-fry over a high heat for a further minute or so. Break the rice up as you go, so everything is combined well. Once the rice is mixed in, add the soy sauce, sprinkle in the chicken stock powder, season with salt and pepper, and stir-fry briefly. Remove from the heat once the flavourings are well blended.

4. Serve on a plate and top with spring onion to finish.

SEAFOOD TIANJIN RICE IN A SAUCE

Serves 1

This recipe stir-fries the topping but not the rice itself, so the flavours and rice only mix as you eat the dish. As with many stir-fried dishes, the cooking time is quick, so there will be no waiting about. If you want to speed it up further, you can use microwaveable pouches of rice, which store well and are a handy store-cupboard ingredient for last-minute suppers.

---

150 grams (5 oz/1 cup) cooked Thai fragrant (jasmine) rice
80 grams (3 oz) frozen seafood mix, thawed
1½ teaspoons cooking sake
½ teaspoon chicken stock powder
½ teaspoon grated ginger
2 medium (US large) eggs
1 tablespoon sesame oil
1½ teaspoons sugar
1 tablespoon rice vinegar
1 tablespoon Japanese soy sauce
120 ml (4 fl oz/½ cup) water
1½ teaspoons cornflour (cornstarch), dissolved in 1½ teaspoons water
Spring onions (scallions), chopped, to garnish

1. If you don't have leftover rice, cook the rice following the packet instructions and set aside. Once the rice is ready, start preparing your additional ingredients. Drain the thawed seafood mix.

2. Put the seafood mix, sake, chicken stock powder and grated ginger into a heat-resistant bowl, cover loosely with cling film (plastic wrap) and heat in a microwave oven (600W) for about 1 minute. Mix and allow to cool. Alternatively, you can bring it to a boil in a saucepan for 3–4 minutes, taking care so it doesn't burn.

3. Crack the eggs into a separate bowl and beat until the yolk and white are thoroughly combined. Add the seafood mixture to the beaten eggs and stir through to mix.

4. Place your cooked rice in a bowl ready for the topping. Heat the sesame oil in a high-sided frying pan or wok over a medium heat. When it is nice and hot, pour in the seafood and egg mixture and stir-fry. When the egg is cooked but still slightly runny, remove it from the heat and spoon it on top of the rice in a bowl.

5. Add the sugar, vinegar, soy sauce, chicken stock powder and water to the same frying pan and heat over a medium heat. Once it comes to a gentle boil, add the dissolved cornflour. Keep stirring until it thickens.
6. Drizzle the sauce over the seafood-topped rice and sprinkle with chopped spring onions.

SALTED SALMON GARLIC FRIED RICE

Serves 2

The richness and plumpness of salmon flesh is the perfect bedfellow for the plain contrast of rice, and when stir-fried the two are a match made in heaven. Japanese fried-rice dishes often use short grain japonica varieties, which are slightly stickier than the Thai fragrant rice used here. You can switch them if you are seeking a thicker, more held-together texture.

---

300 grams (10½ oz/1½ cups) cooked Thai fragrant (jasmine) rice
1 clove garlic
5 spring onions (scallions)
80 grams (3 oz) salmon fillet
1 teaspoon sea salt
1½ teaspoons cooking sake
1 medium (US large) egg
1 tablespoon olive oil
Salt and pepper, to taste

1. If you don't have leftover rice, after cooking the rice following the packet instructions, set the pan aside. Once the rice is ready, start preparing your additional ingredients. Slice the garlic clove thinly. Trim the roots from the spring onions and chop the stalks into small pieces.

2. Place the salmon on a heat-resistant plate and sprinkle with the sea salt and sake. Cover loosely with cling film (plastic wrap) and heat in a microwave oven (600W) for 3 minutes. Alternatively, you can cook it in a shallow frying pan over a medium heat, turning it over after 2 minutes to cook both sides. Once cooled, remove the skin and any bones from the fillet and flake the meat gently with your fingers or a fork.

3. Beat the egg in a small bowl until the yolk and the white are thoroughly combined. Add the olive oil and garlic to a high-sided frying pan or wok over a low heat. Fry the garlic until golden, then remove it from the pan with a slotted spoon to a small plate.

4. Reheat the same frying pan over a medium heat, then tip in the beaten egg and mix vigorously until soft cooked. Add the rice, salted salmon and a pinch of salt and pepper and stir-fry for about 2 minutes. As you stir-fry, loosen the rice with chopsticks or a wooden spatula so all the grains separate. Add the spring onions and stir-fry for a further minute.

5. Serve on plates and top with the garlic slices.

FRIED RICE

PORK AND KIMCHI FRIED RICE

Serves 2

Fermented foods are having a resurgence due to their health benefits for the microbiome in our digestive tract, where they help balance the natural, good microorganisms. If you are struggling to find ideas for adding these incredible foods to your diet, then this recipe is a must. The sweet and sour tanginess of kimchi cuts through the richness of the pork and egg for a deliciously balanced stir-fry.

---

300 grams (10½ oz/1½ cups) cooked Thai fragrant (jasmine) rice
100 grams (3½ oz) pork belly
100 grams (3½ oz/½ cup) kimchi
1 medium (US large) egg
1 teaspoon sesame oil
2 teaspoons Japanese soy sauce
Salt and pepper, to taste
4 spring onions (scallions), finely chopped

1. If you don't have leftover rice, after cooking the rice following the packet instructions, set the pan aside. Once the rice is ready, start preparing your additional ingredients. Thinly slice the pork and cut into bite-sized pieces. Scoop the kimchi pieces out of the jar and snip them into bite-sized pieces with scissors. Crack the egg into a bowl and beat until the yolk and white are thoroughly combined.

2. Heat your sesame oil in a high-sided frying pan or wok over a medium heat. Once it is hot, pour in the beaten egg and stir vigorously. Remove the frying pan or wok from the heat when the egg is roughly half-cooked (still a little loose). Pour into a dish and set aside.

3. Now return the pan to a medium heat, and once it is hot again, add the meat pieces and cook for 5–7 minutes until the pork is cooked through. Add the kimchi to the pan and stir-fry briefly. After about a minute, tip in the rice and stir-fry while breaking

it up with chopsticks or a wooden spatula to separate the grains. Pour in the soy sauce, season with salt and pepper and mix.

4. Add the egg back to the pan and stir-fry quickly (another minute at most).

5. Serve into two bowls and sprinkle with the chopped spring onions.

FRIED RICE

FRIED BEEF WITH SUNNY SIDE UP EGG

Serves 2

Fried rice is thought to have first been made in Yangzhou, a Chinese city close to the river Yangtze. They take their cooking seriously and even have a recommendation for the amount of colour in a fried-rice dish. Browns from caramelized meats, the pink of seafood, and flecks of bright green spring onion or the golden yolk of an egg are all encouraged to make friends with each other in the wok.

---

300 grams (10½ oz/1½ cups) cooked Thai fragrant (jasmine) rice
¼ large white onion
1 bunch of chives
120 grams (4 oz) beef strips
1½ teaspoons olive oil
2 medium (US large) eggs
1½ teaspoons sesame oil

Marinade
1 tablespoon cooking sake
1 teaspoon sugar
1 tablespoon Japanese soy sauce
½ tablespoon gochujang (Korean red chilli paste)
½ teaspoon grated ginger

1. If you don't have leftover rice, after cooking the rice following the packet instructions, set the pan aside. Once the rice is ready, start preparing your additional ingredients. Slice the onion in half lengthways and, with the flat side down, cut diagonally into 1-cm (½-inch) pieces. Trim the roots of the chives and cut the green stalks into 3-cm (1¼-inch) pieces.

2. To make a marinade, add the sake, sugar, soy sauce, *gochujang* and grated ginger to a medium-sized bowl and mix together well. Add the beef strips and onion slices to the same bowl and mix until well combined.

3. Heat the olive oil in a high-sided frying pan or wok over a medium heat until the oil is nice and hot. Gently drop in the marinated beef and onion mixture. Stir-fry for 3–4 minutes until the beef is cooked through and the onion has softened.

4. Tip in the pre-cooked rice and stir-fry for another couple of minutes, breaking the rice up, so that the grains are nice and

FRIED RICE

separated and well combined with the other ingredients. Add the chopped chives and stir-fry briefly for a few seconds further.

5. Serve it into two bowls and then quickly fry your eggs – sunny side up – in the frying pan. Gently scoop them out and place them on top of each bowl, then drizzle with sesame oil.

SCALLOP FRIED RICE WITH GARLIC & BUTTER

Serves 2

The sweet, juicy, plump delicacy of scallops is a real indulgence. Sometimes, because of the sweetness of their flesh, they are referred to as "sea candy". In Japan, there are four main regions that are plentiful in these seafood wonders, and they are grilled, seared and shallow-fried, or enjoyed raw as sashimi, because their quality is second to none. In this dish, the butter adds a further level of indulgence, while the soy sauce contrasts perfectly with the scallop flavour.

---

300 grams (10½ oz/1½ cups) cooked Thai fragrant (jasmine) rice
3 Savoy cabbage leaves
1 clove garlic
2 spring onions (scallions), to garnish
20 grams (¾ oz/1½ tablespoons) salted butter
1 tablespoon Japanese soy sauce
Salt and pepper, to taste
1 tablespoon olive oil
80 grams (3 oz) baby scallops

1. If you don't have leftover rice, after cooking the rice following the packet instructions, set the pan aside. Once the rice is ready, start preparing your additional ingredients. Cut the cabbage leaves into bite-sized pieces and thinly slice the garlic, chop your spring onions, and set all aside.

2. Mash the salted butter with the soy sauce seasoned with salt and pepper in a small bowl.

3. Heat the olive oil in a high-sided frying pan or wok over a medium heat and, when hot, add the garlic and quickly fry (but take care not to allow it to burn). When the garlic is fragrant, add the cabbage and stir-fry until it softens. Tip in the cooked rice and stir-fry for a further few minutes, being sure to break the rice up delicately with chopsticks or a wooden spatula, so the grains separate and the oil coats them.

4. Add the baby scallops and stir-fry together for a couple of minutes until the scallops lose their translucency. At this point, spoon in the butter blend and stir-fry together for a minute to mix it through.

5. Serve in two bowls and sprinkle with the chopped spring onions for a delicious, light supper.

MACKEREL FRIED RICE

Serves 2

Mackerel features in a lot of Japanese dishes. It is a versatile fish, supremely tasty and bursting in beneficial fish oils. *Shime saba* is a specially cured, uncooked Japanese version that can be eaten as sashimi or over sushi. Mackerel fillets often make up part of a bento box assortment. Although you could use fresh mackerel here, I use canned mackerel for this recipe, not only for its ease and affordability, but because the intensity of its salty flavour adds more dimension to the rice, plus being already cooked, the stir-fry time required is very short.

---

300 grams (10½ oz/1½ cups) cooked Thai fragrant (jasmine) rice
120 grams (4 oz) canned mackerel
⅓ of a bag kale
2 medium (US large) eggs
1 tablespoon olive oil
2 teaspoons Japanese soy sauce
Salt and pepper, to taste
Dried bonito flakes, to garnish

1. If you don't have leftover rice, after cooking the rice following the packet instructions, set the pan aside. Once the rice is ready, start preparing your additional ingredients. Drain the liquid from the canned mackerel. Chop the kale into 1-cm (½-inch) pieces. Put the rice in a bowl, crack the eggs into it and mix the yolks and whites until thoroughly combined.

2. Heat olive oil in a high-sided frying pan or wok over a medium heat. When the oil is hot, add the canned mackerel, breaking it up a little, and chopped kale, then stir-fry for about 2 minutes.

3. Tip in your cooked rice and stir-fry for 3–4 minutes, moving the rice with a chopstick or wooden spatula to separate the grains. Add the soy sauce and season with salt and pepper, then stir-fry together for a further minute.

4. Once ready, serve onto plates and top with a sprinkle of bonito flakes.

EGG SOUP FRIED RICE

Serves 2

Just as the French have *Isles flottantes* – a beautiful, soft meringue desert where the "islands" float in a soup of crème anglaise – so this classic Chinese dish features an island of fried rice. The thick, creamy egg soup goes well with fluffy fried rice, making it a great comfort food or a warming dish to make on colder days.

---

300 grams (10½ oz/1½ cups) cooked Thai fragrant (jasmine) rice
45 grams (1½ oz/4 medium) spring onions (scallions)
1 clove garlic
2 medium (US large) eggs
1½ teaspoons olive oil
100 grams (3½ oz) minced (ground) pork
½ teaspoon salt
Pepper, to taste
½ teaspoon chicken stock powder
400 ml (14 fl oz/1⅔ cups) water
1½ tablespoons cornflour (cornstarch), dissolved in 1½ tablespoons water
1 teaspoon sesame oil

1. If you don't have leftover rice, after cooking the rice following the packet instructions, set the pan aside with the lid on. Prepare your vegetables: finely chop the spring onions and cut the garlic in half lengthways then finely slice it. Crack your eggs into a small bowl and mix until thoroughly combined.
2. Heat the oil in a high-sided frying pan or wok over a low heat. Add your garlic and, when it becomes fragrant, tip in the pork. Raise the heat to medium and stir-fry; keep it moving until the meat changes colour and becomes pale all over.
3. Add the spring onions and stir-fry for around 1½ minutes until they are soft. Add the rice and stir-fry for a further couple of minutes, breaking the rice down gently with chopsticks or a wooden spoon to separate the grains. Season to taste.
4. Put the stock powder and water into a small saucepan over a high heat. When it comes to the boil, add the cornflour, reduce to a simmer and stir until it thickens. Pour in the eggs, stirring continually so they disperse throughout, and simmer until they are set. Finally, stir through the sesame oil to finish the broth.
5. Mound the rice in the middle of two deep bowls and pour the egg soup round the fried rice like a moat.

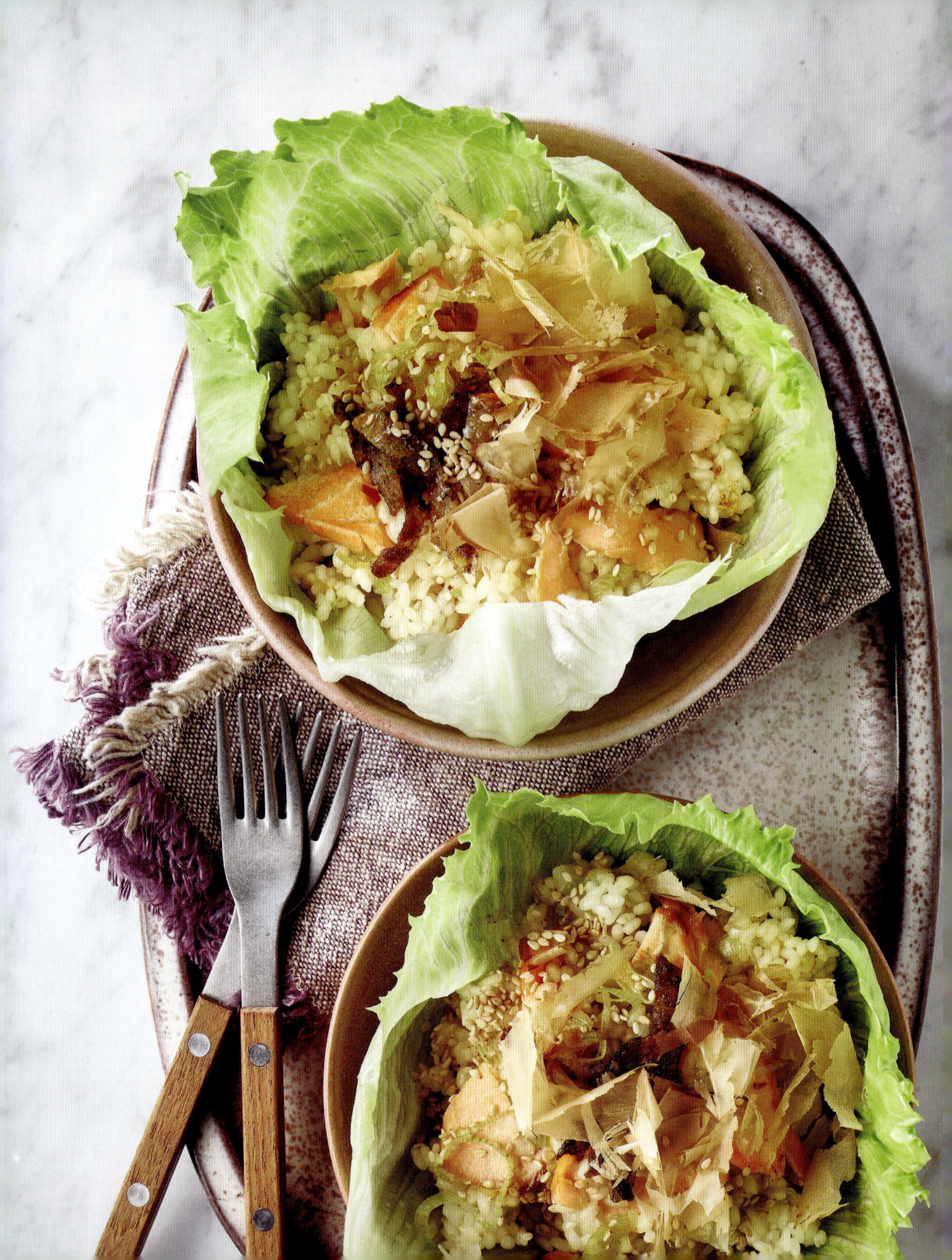

TAKIKOMI GOHAN HOTATE (SAVOURY RICE)

Japanese rice is a staple accompaniment to most meals and is the foundation of the ubiquitous sushi rolls. Although sushi rice is flavoured with a little rice wine vinegar, sugar and salt, a bowl of plain rice can be fairly bland without the addition of other flavours. You can elevate a bowl of rice by shaking over the dried savouriness of *furikake* flakes or nori seaweed, or by adding salty strips of smoked salmon, a squeeze of wasabi, a sprinkle of sesame seeds or zesty *tsukemono* pickles. But if you really want to build savoury rice into a main meal, try *takikomi gohan hotate*. These are rice dishes that combine Japanese seasoning and other ingredients – vegetables, fish and meat. No longer just an accompaniment, these recipes add texture and flavour, transforming a rice bowl into a main meal.

GINGER OCTOPUS RICE

Serves 2 as a main dish • Serves 4 as a side dish

Seafood and rice are a match made in heaven and, of course, a staple of Japanese cuisine. Here, the tentacles of octopus add a meaty texture to the flavour-infused rice. For this recipe, we have used a rice cooker, as it really helps infuse all of the flavours together and adds to the simplicity of cooking this dish.

---

100 grams (3½ oz) frozen, cooked octopus tentacles (purchase from Asian stores)
1 thumb-sized piece of fresh root ginger
300 grams (10½ oz/1½ cups) japonica rice
2 tablespoons dark soy sauce
2 tablespoons mirin
1 tablespoon cooking sake
400 ml (14 fl oz/1⅗ cups) water

1. Defrost the octopus in cold water for 20 minutes. Cut the tentacles into 1-cm (½-inch) pieces. Prepare the ginger by peeling or scraping away the skin and cutting the root lengthways into fine matchsticks.

2. Rinse your rice for a few minutes under cold running water in a sieve, then tip the rinsed rice, soy sauce, mirin and sake into the rice cooker pot. Pour the water into the rice cooker and mix the pot contents briefly with a spoon.

3. Spread the octopus pieces and ginger matchsticks evenly across the top of the rice and clamp the lid on.

4. Set the rice cooker to a high heat setting until steam is released, then turn the heat down low for 10 minutes – do not open the lid. Now turn the heat high again but just for 1 minute, then turn the heat off completely and leave the pot with the lid still on for a further 10 minutes.

5. Mix the octopus and ginger through the flavoured rice and serve as a meal in itself.

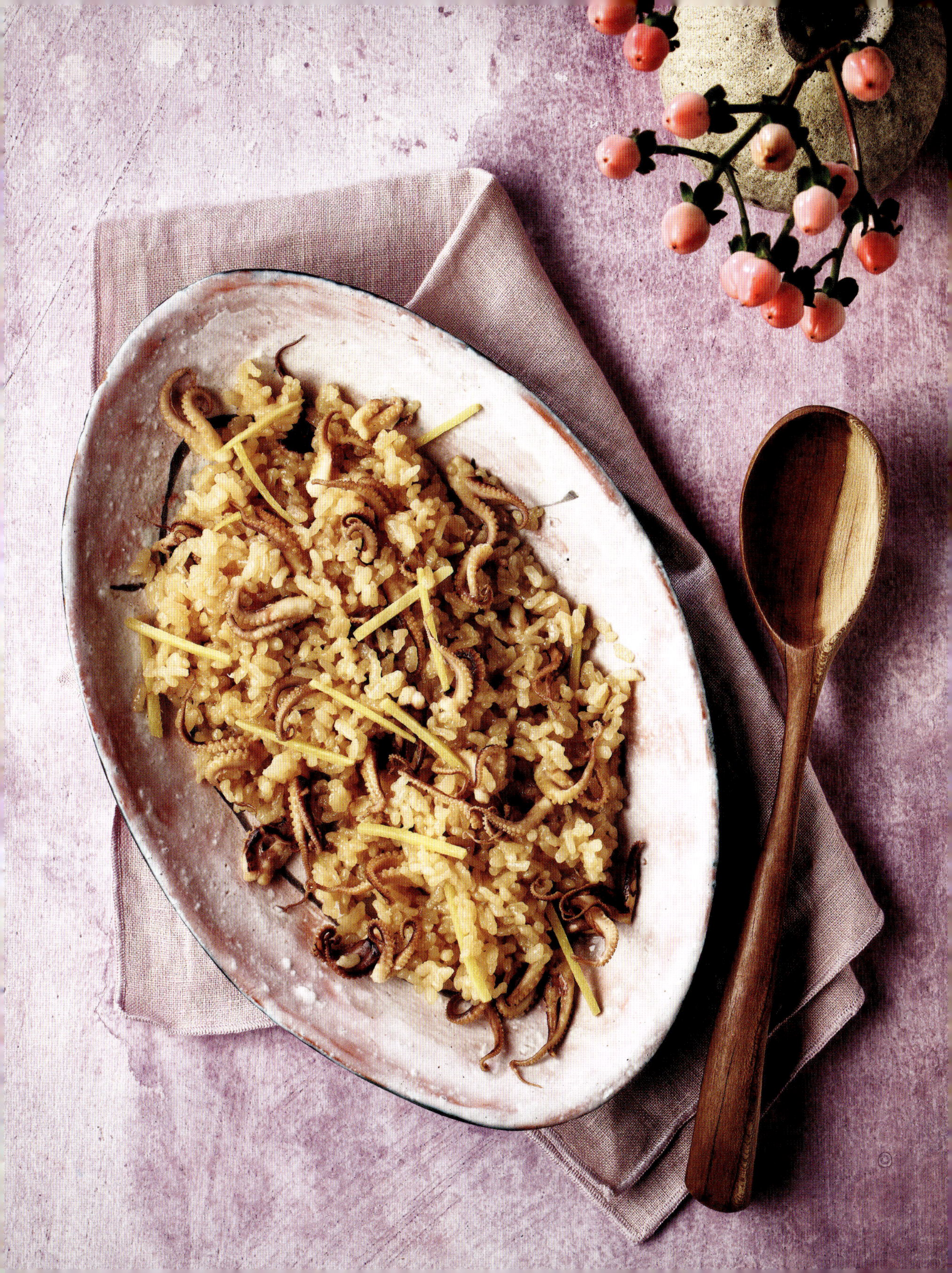

SWEETCORN BUTTER RICE

Serves 2 as a main dish • Serves 4 as a side dish

If you are a fan of the sweet crunch of corn on the cob, this dish is for you. Enjoy it as a side dish or a main. The instructions for this recipe are for using a rice cooker. Adding butter to finish will give this rice a richness that enhances both the savouriness of the dish and the flavour. For a healthier version, try making it with brown rice.

---

1 sweetcorn cob
300 grams (10½ oz/1½ cups) japonica rice or Thai fragrant (jasmine) rice
2 tablespoons cooking sake
½ teaspoon salt
400 ml (14 fl oz/1⅔ cups) water
20 grams (¾ oz/1½ tablespoons) salted butter
1 tablespoon fresh parsley, chopped

1. Cut the corn in half midway, so you have two shorter pieces. Stand each one vertically, then insert a knife near the cob and scrape down to shave off the edible kernels. Don't throw away the cobs, as they will be used to add extra flavour in the pot.

2. Add the rice, sake and salt to the rice cooker pot. Now pour in the water. Mix gently, then flatten the mixture in the pan before spreading the corn kernels over the rice. Place the hulled corn cobs on top of the kernels.

3. Set the pot to a high heat setting and cook until steam is released, then turn the heat down to low for 10 minutes – do not open the lid. Now turn the heat back to high just for 1 minute, then turn it completely off and leave the pot with the lid still on for a further 10 minutes.

4. When the corn and rice is cooked and tender, remove the corn cobs, add in the butter and mix gently.

5. Divide between two bowls and sprinkle with a generous amount of chopped parsley.

COCONUT CHICKEN RICE

Serves 2 as a main dish

This rice dish does its cooking in the oven, making it an easy-to-prepare-and-leave meal that is great to make with kids and is suited to busy lifestyles. This dish is inspired by *doria*, a very popular Japanese, pilaf-style dish covered in béchamel and baked for unctuousness. This version features coconut milk to create the creamy, delicious finish.

---

2 boneless, skinless chicken thighs
2 whole chicken wings
2 teaspoons curry powder
1 teaspoon salt
½ teaspoon black pepper
2 tablespoons vegetable oil
½ medium white onion, roughly chopped
½ green bell pepper, roughly chopped
1 teaspoon very finely chopped garlic
1 teaspoon very finely chopped ginger
360 grams (12½ oz/2 cups) basmati rice
1 tablespoon tomato purée (paste)
240 ml (8½ fl oz/1 cup) chicken stock
240 ml (8½ fl oz/1 cup) coconut milk
Coriander (cilantro), to garnish

1. Preheat the oven to 180°C (350°F). Cut the thighs into thirds and divide the wings into wing tips and ends. Season the meat with the curry powder, salt and pepper.

2. Heat the oil in an oven-safe pot over a medium heat, add the chicken and cook on both sides for a few minutes until browned (they don't need to be cooked through as they will be finished off later), then set aside on a plate.

3. Add the onion, green pepper, garlic and ginger to the pot and fry until soft. Add the uncooked rice to the vegetables, stir-frying until it goes translucent. Now, add the tomato purée and fry for a further minute or so. When the spices, vegetables and rice are well mixed, pour the chicken stock and coconut milk into the pot. Taste and adjust the salt and pepper if necessary.

4. Tip the chicken into the liquid and bring the pot to a boil. Cover with a lid, place in the preheated oven and cook for 20 minutes. Alternatively, put the lid on the pot and cook over a low heat on the hob (stove) for 20 minutes until all the liquid has evaporated.

5. Once the rice is tender and the liquid has been mostly absorbed, serve into bowls with a sprinkling of coriander to taste.

SWEET POTATO BUTTER RICE

Serves 2 as a main dish • Serves 4 as a side dish

Sweet potatoes are a firm favourite in Japanese cuisine, and the vibrant hues of this root vegetable are a familiar part of home cooking. Known as *satsuma-imo*, they are grown throughout the country, and digging them up is an autumn tradition for many schoolchildren. This dish utilizes a rice cooker, which makes preparing the rice and sweet potatoes a one-pot task and cuts down on cleaning up. The saltiness of the butter added at the end balances the caramel sweetness of the potatoes.

---

120 grams (4 oz/1 small) sweet potato
300 grams (10½ oz/1½ cups) japonica rice
½ teaspoon kelp powder
½ teaspoon salt
400 ml (14 fl oz/1⅔ cups) water
20 grams (¾ oz/1½ tablespoons) salted butter

1. The sweet potato will be lightly mashed at a later stage. If you like a rustic mash, you can leave the peel on, but if you prefer a smoother texture, peel the sweet potato. With or without the peel, cut the sweet potato into quarters, then soak the quarters in water for about 15 minutes and drain.

2. Rinse your rice under cold running water in a sieve and, after a couple of minutes rinsing, tip the rice into the rice cooker. Sprinkle the kelp powder and the salt over the pot of rice and then pour in the water. Mix the water, rice, kelp powder and salt through gently, and then level off the rice to form a flat bed, on which you can then spread the sweet potatoes.

3. Set your rice cooker to the settings required for cooking that quantity of rice and let it do its work. When the rice is cooked, open the lid of your rice cooker, add in the butter and mix while gently breaking the now soft sweet potatoes into the rice mixture.

4. Serve in bowls for the ultimate comfort food.

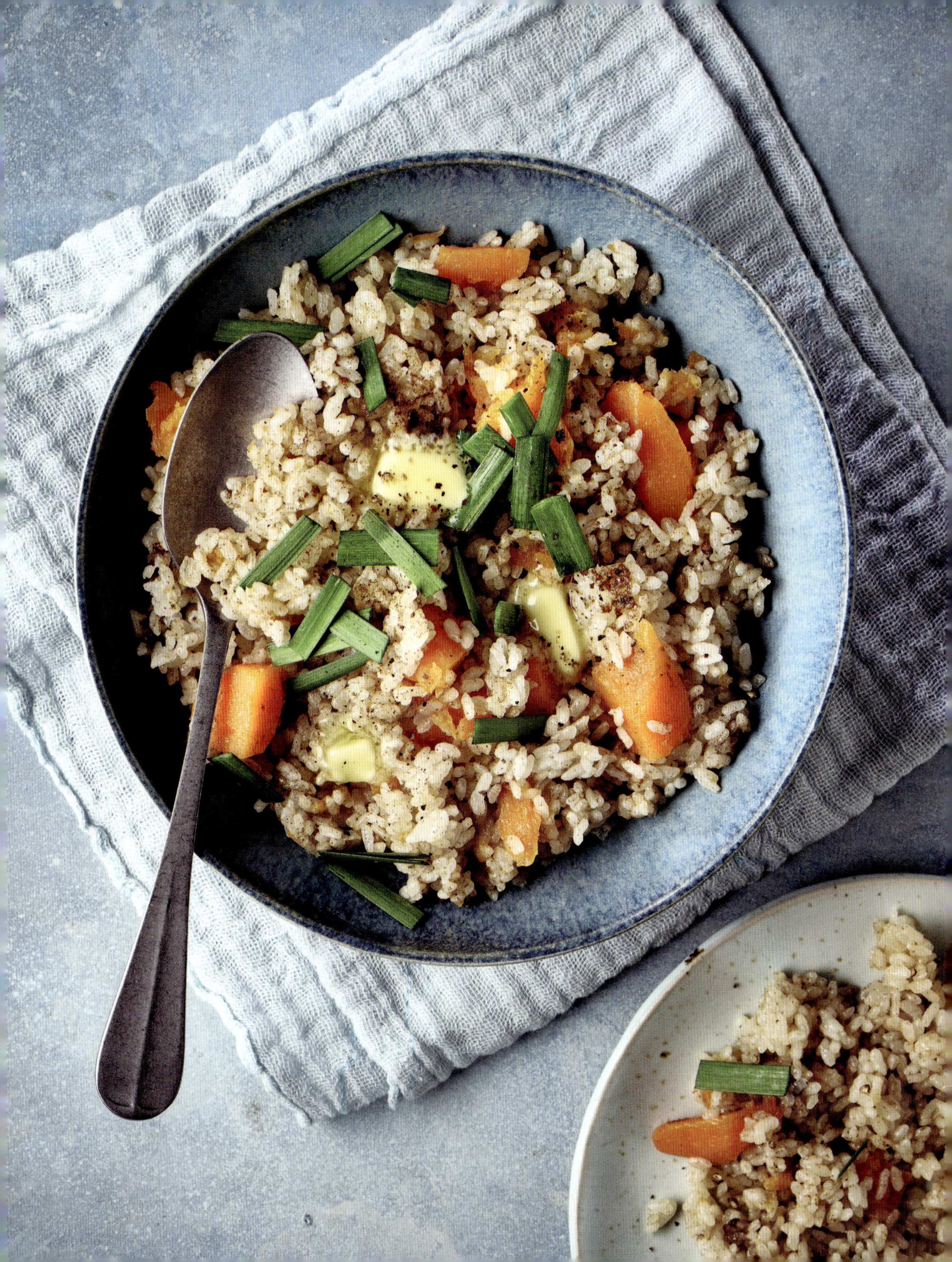

SALMON & FLAVORED LEEK LETTUCE BOWL

Serves 4

This delicious summery lunch utilizes a crisp lettuce leaf as its serving bowl, making it lovely to hand round at summer gatherings or whenever you fancy a refreshing snack. The filling is served just warm so as not to wilt the lettuce bowls.

---

350 grams (12⅜ oz/1¾ cups) japonica rice or Thai fragrant (jasmine) rice
400 ml (14 fl oz/1⅔ cups)
2 teaspoons sea salt
1 medium-sized leek, white part only
½ thumb-sized piece of fresh root ginger
120 ml (4 fl oz/½ cup) sesame oil
2 tablespoons sesame oil
3 tablespoons miso
1 tablespoon mirin
5 grams (⅛ oz/⅓ cup) dried bonito flakes
120 grams (4 oz) salmon fillet
4 iceberg lettuce leaves (1 per "bowl")
1½ tablespoons toasted white sesame seeds

1. Prepare your rice by rinsing it under cold running water in a sieve for a couple of minutes and drain well. Put it into a medium-sized saucepan and add the water, then leave to sit and soak in the pan for at least 30 minutes.

2. Sprinkle the salt into the saucepan with the soaking rice and stir. Put the lid on and bring it to the boil over a high heat, then turn the heat down to a low simmer. Cook over a low heat for 10 minutes, then turn the heat off and leave it to rest with the lid on for a further 12 minutes. This dish is served warm but not piping hot.

3. Meanwhile, finely chop the white part of the leek and grate the ginger. Heat the sesame oil in a frying pan over a medium heat. Add the leek and ginger and stir-fry for 1 minute. Now add the miso and mirin and stir through the leeks for a further minute or so. The leeks will now be translucent and you can sprinkle the bonito flakes over, mix and then turn off the heat and set the frying pan aside to cool for about 15 minutes.

4. Now grill your salmon fillet for 5–7 minutes on both sides, then leave to cool down a little before gently flaking the fillets using a fork. Pour the leek sauce over the salmon flakes and mix into the rice.

5. Use your lettuce leave as bowls and fill them with the leek salmon and rice mixture. Sprinkle with toasted sesame seeds and enjoy .

MUSHROOM & ANCHOVY RICE

Serves 2 as a main dish • Serves 4 as a side dish

Mushrooms are now understood to be a superfood and each variety has different particular benefits with it. Japan has a long-running culture of foraging, making mushrooms a go-to ingredient. Here, we combine three of the most popular Japanese mushrooms in one dish. With its lemony aroma, it's a perfect dish for when you don't have much of an appetite.

300 grams (10½ oz/1½ cups) japonica rice or Thai fragrant (jasmine) rice
360 ml (12½ fl oz/1½ cups) water
1 unwaxed lemon
100 grams (3½ oz) shiitake mushrooms
50 grams (1¾ oz) shimeji mushrooms
50 grams (1¾ oz) oyster mushrooms
50 grams (1¾ oz) canned anchovies
2 tablespoons dark soy sauce
1 tablespoon cooking sake
1 tablespoon olive oil
A pinch of salt
A pinch of black pepper (optional)
5–6 chives, chopped, to garnish
Sesame seeds, to garnish

1. Rinse the rice under cold running water in a sieve for a couple of minutes and drain it well. Place it in a medium-sized saucepan, add the water, then leave to soak for at least 30 minutes.

2. Meanwhile, cut half the lemon into thin slices. Prepare all of the mushrooms by wiping them clean, ensuring there is no grit or grime in them, and chopping them into small pieces. Slice the anchovies into 1-cm (½-inch) pieces.

3. Gently mix the mushrooms, soy sauce, sake and olive oil in a bowl, evenly coating the mushroom pieces with the mixture.

4. Sprinkle salt and pepper, if using, into the soaking rice and stir. Now, in this order, add the anchovies and mushrooms and top with the sliced lemon. Put the lid on and bring it to the boil over a high heat, then turn the heat down and simmer for 10 minutes.

5. Turn the heat off and leave to rest with the lid on for 12 minutes. Once ready, open the lid and remove the lemon slices. Squeeze 1 tablespoon of lemon juice from the remaining half lemon and drizzle it over the rice and mushrooms and mix it through well.

6. Spoon the flavoured rice onto plates and sprinkle with some chopped chive and sesame seeds.

TAKIKOMI GOHAN HOTATE

HEALTHY BREAKFAST RICE

Serves 2 as a breakfast dish

A Japanese breakfast looks completely different to Western versions and is considered among the healthiest ways to start the day. Full of protein and slow-burn carbohydrates, it will provide energy for many hours, reducing the temptation to reach for sugary snacks. A traditional Japanese breakfast comprises 6 to 8 dishes, but this savoury rice – a delicious breakfast that's made in minutes and is packed with nutrients – will give you many of the same benefits without the need to create multiple dishes, making it perfect for busy mornings.

---

200 grams (7 oz/1 cup) brown rice or a microwaveable packet
5 grams (⅛ oz/2 tablespoons) dried wakame seaweed
1 tablespoon dark soy sauce
1 teaspoon sesame oil
1 teaspoon mirin

1. Cook your brown rice according to packet instructions, then set aside and allow it to cool slightly so it is warm. Alternatively, you can use a sachet of precooked brown rice to speed things up: simply microwave for a couple of minutes before you are ready to eat.
2. Soak the dried wakame in a suitable amount of water for 3–4 minutes to rehydrate it. Drain the water and gently squeeze the seaweed. If the seaweed pieces are too big, chop them more finely so they are comfortable to eat and will mix better through the rice dish.
3. Put the chopped seaweed into a small bowl and add in the soy sauce, sesame oil and mirin. Mix well, then set aside for 5 minutes to let the flavours combine.
4. Now mix the with the warm brown rice, stirring everything through so all the flavours combine, and serve.

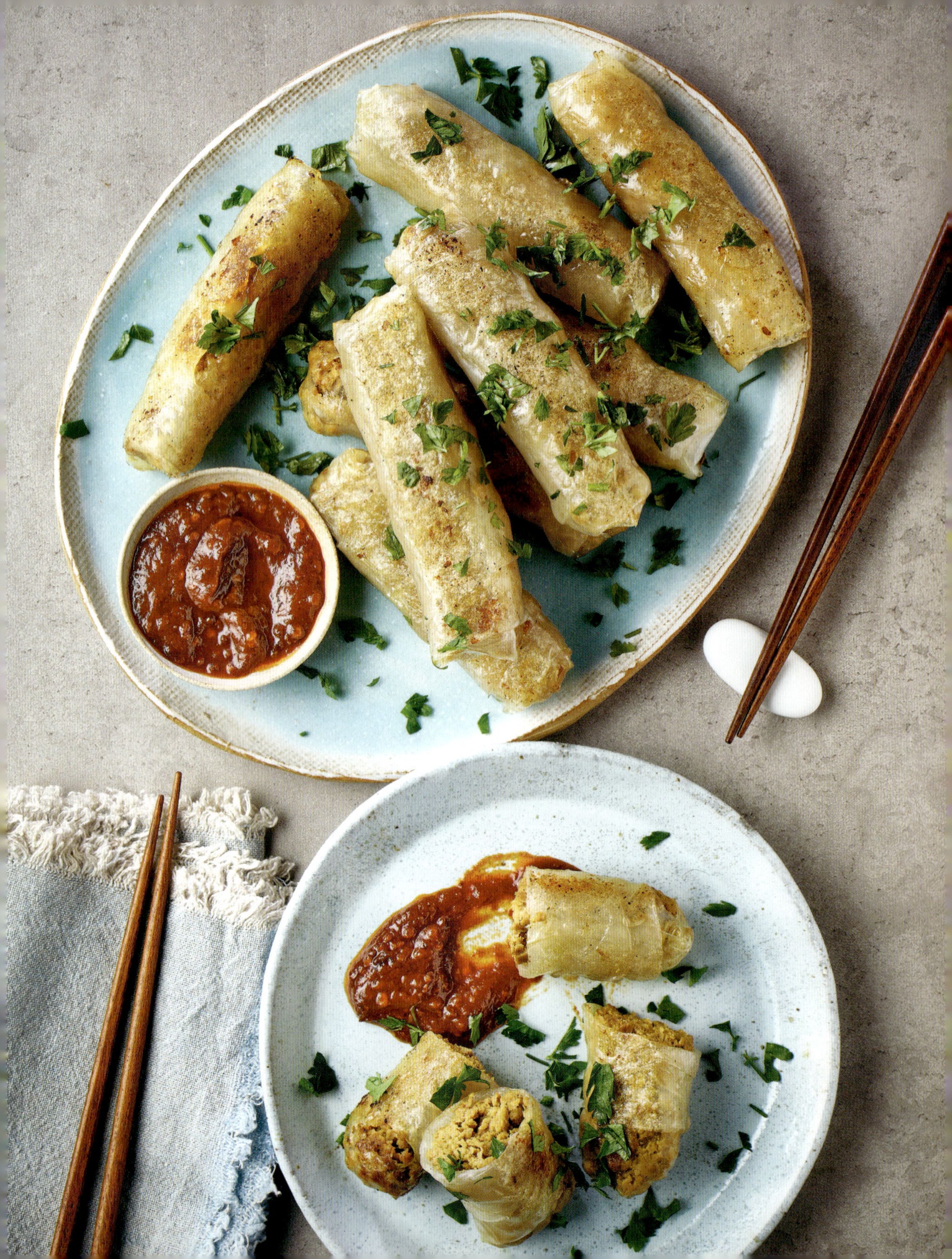

RICE PAPER

This versatile ingredient is used in Asian cuisine to wrap tasty fillings, in much the same way as bread or pastry act as containers for handy Western meals. First known as "paper of Xuancheng", after the area in China where it was created and produced, it is now easy to find in most supermarkets or Asian food stores. Rice paper is an excellent low-calorie, low-sodium and low-fat way to enjoy tasty fillings. There is a knack to the rolling technique, but once you have mastered the art, there will be no end to the fillings and flavours you can build. Rice paper is also a traditional wrapper for sweet treats, and you will find some here to make and enjoy.

THAI / VIETNAMESE-STYLE SPRING ROLLS

Makes 6

This recipe blends the delicious pork and mushroom centre of Vietnamese spring rolls, called *cha gio*, with the vermicelli heart of Thai spring rolls, or *poh piah*. Vermicelli, or glass noodles, as they are often called, fill the centre of these rolls, giving them substance and bringing the other filling ingredients together. Enjoy these dipped in a peanut sauce. In this recipe, I shallow-fry them, but you could easily cook them in an air fryer instead. Simply brush the rice paper lightly with olive oil, space out in a single layer in the air fryer basket and cook for 12–14 minutes at 200°C (400°F).

---

50 grams (2 oz) firm tofu
125 grams (4 oz/2 leaves) Savoy cabbage
50 grams (2 oz/1 small) carrot
30 grams (1 oz) enoki mushrooms
3 stalks Chinese chives
1 clove garlic
30 grams (1 oz) pea starch vermicelli
1½ teaspoons rice bran oil
Pinch of chilli powder
50 grams (2 oz) minced (ground) pork
6 sheets of rice paper
Vegetable oil, for shallow-frying

1. Heat the firm tofu in its liquid in the microwave oven (500W) for 2 minutes. Drain and cut the block into thin strips.

2. Cut the cabbage leaves into strips and the carrot into thin batons. Separate the stalks of the enoki mushrooms. Snip the Chinese chives into 3-cm (1¼-inch) lengths. Finely chop the garlic.

3. Now make a sauce by mixing together the Thai soy sauce, pepper, oyster sauce, fish sauce, sugar and sesame oil in a small bowl.

4. Boil the vermicelli in plenty of water for 4 minutes. After boiling, rinse under running water and drain thoroughly.

5. Heat the rice bran oil in a frying pan over medium-high heat, add the chopped garlic, chilli powder and minced pork, and stir-fry until the garlic becomes fragrant. Add the cabbage, carrot, enoki

Sauce
½ tablespoon Thai soy sauce or light soy sauce
Freshly ground black pepper (5 turns of the mill)
4 teaspoons oyster sauce
½ teaspoon fish sauce
1 teaspoon sugar
1 teaspoon sesame oil

mushrooms, Chinese chives and firm tofu, and stir-fry for 2–3 minutes until cooked through.

6. Add the drained vermicelli and stir-fry lightly for 1 minute. Add the sauce and stir-fry for a further 1 minute, making sure it is well mixed. Set aside to cool.

7. Make the rolls: one at a time soak each piece of rice paper in warm water (about 40°C/104°F) for 20–30 seconds to rehydrate. Place each rehydrated rice paper sheet onto a chopping board, arranging them in a diamond shape. Divide the ingredient mixture among the 6 sheets, placing the mixture slightly below the centre of each sheet.

8. Now fold up the bottom of the rice paper, then fold in the left and right sides of the rice paper. Finish by rolling the sheet from bottom to top. Set aside for a few minutes to allow the rolls to dry a little so they don't spit when fried.

9. Put the vegetable oil into a high-sided frying pan over medium heat. When the temperature reaches 150–160°C (300–325°F), add the spring rolls and fry slowly and for 10–15 minutes to ensure everything is cooked through. Fried spring rolls tend to stick together in the pan so keep them slightly apart.

10. Once cooked, transfer to a small plate and cut in half if you like.

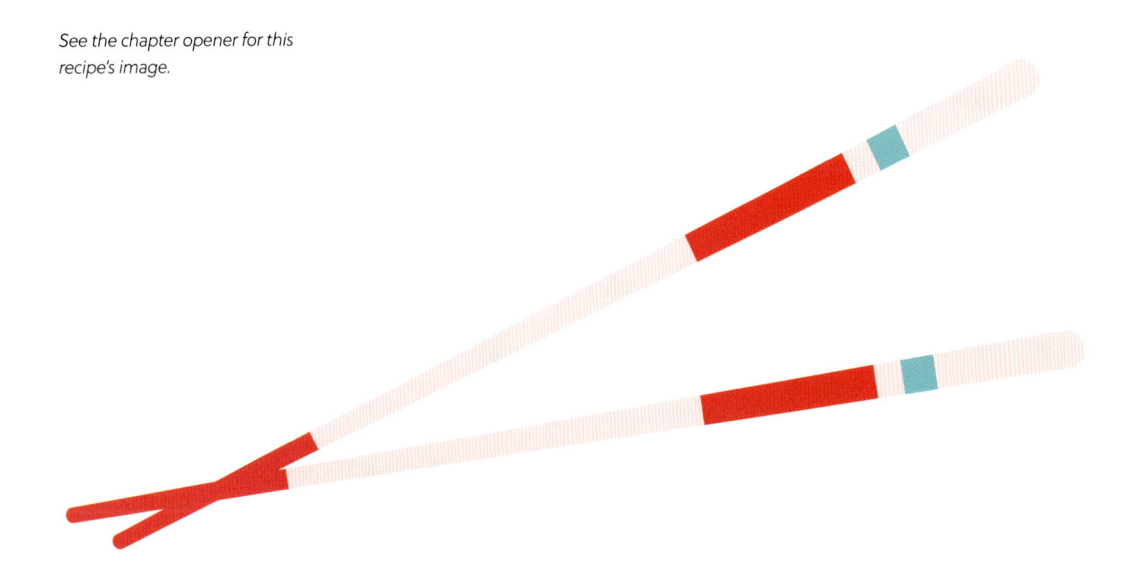

See the chapter opener for this recipe's image.

SALMON & AVOCADO PAPER ROLL

Serves 2 as a snack • Serves 1 as a main meal

Smoked salmon and avocado are a modern culinary couple; you won't believe how simple it is to create them yourself. This recipe also provides much needed inspiration as an alternative to a lunchtime sandwich when working from home.

6 sheets of rice paper
½ avocado
12 smoked salmon slices
12 baby gem lettuce leaves
6 thin slices Cheddar cheese
2½ tablespoons mayonnaise
1 teaspoon wasabi paste
1 teaspoon Japanese soy sauce

1. To rehydrate the dried rice paper, wet some kitchen paper towel and place it on a chopping board. Now soak each piece of rice paper in warm water (about 40°C/104°F) for 20–30 seconds. When it becomes floppy, remove it from the bowl, shake it gently to get rid of the excess water and place it on the damp kitchen paper towel (this way the rice paper stays moist).

2. Halve your avocado, then peel and cut one half into slices lengthways (leave the stone in the other half to store it wrapped in cling film/plastic wrap in the fridge).

3. Taking a sheet of rice paper, put 2 slices of the smoked salmon and 2 slices of avocado in the middle of the sheet. Next, place 2 gem lettuce leaves on top, followed by a slice of cheese.

4. Starting from the side nearest to you, roll the rice paper and ingredients slowly and tightly in one go, as if you were making sushi rolls, stopping two thirds of the way.

5. Now, fold both open sides of the rice paper inwards, tucking them into the roll and finish rolling the cylinder up.

6. Mix the mayonnaise, wasabi and soy sauce to make a dipping sauce.

7. Stack on a plate as you go and then enjoy with a dipping sauce – lemon mayonnaise works beautifully.

MATCHA PAPER-WRAPPED CHEESECAKE

Makes 3

These rice paper-wrapped cheesecakes require virtually no cooking. Instead, the fridge helps set the interior of these delicious, Oreo-filled, creamy treats.

---

50 grams (2 oz/scant ¼ cup) cream cheese
1 teaspoon matcha powder, plus extra to decorate
20 grams (¾ oz/1½ tablespoons) caster (superfine) sugar
200 ml (7 fl oz/scant 1 cup) double (heavy) cream
3 Oreo biscuits
3 sheets of rice paper
1 teaspoon sticky (glutinous) rice flour
3 strawberries, stalks removed and sliced

See overleaf for step-by-step images.

1. Put the cream cheese into a heat-resistant bowl and heat in the microwave (600W) for 20 seconds until soft. Alternatively, put it into a glass bowl and melt it over a saucepan of simmering water.

2. Add the matcha powder, sugar and 1 tablespoon of the cream to the cream cheese, mixing well with a rubber spatula. Gently crush the Oreos and mix in too. Pour in the remaining cream, place on top of a bowl of ice and whip with a whisk or hand mixer until 80 per cent stiff. Seal the bowl with cling film (plastic wrap), pressing down to remove any air. Remove from the ice bowl and chill in the refrigerator.

3. Soak each piece of rice paper in warm water for 20–30 seconds, then place into a 6–7cm (2½–2¾ inch) diameter cup to create a small bowl. Lightly brush the interior with rice flour. Flip the bowl over so that the flour-coated side is facing down in the cup.

4. Fill each bowl with cream mixture and add sliced strawberries. Pull the rice paper edges toward the centre to seal the contents and snip off any excess.

5. Gently tip the parcels out of the cup so the pulled together sides are facing down plate. Sprinkle with matcha powder to finish.

STEP BY STEP: MATCHA PAPER-WRAPPED CHEESECAKE

STEP BY STEP: PRAWN WONTON SOUP

PRAWN WONTON SOUP

Serves 2

In Cantonese, *wonton* translates as "cloud swallow", and who can resist these delightful squidgy mouthfuls of savoury delight. Less charmingly, the Mandarin translation is "irregular shaped dumpling" and perhaps that is closer to the truth. The point is, wonton don't have to be perfect or look great – they just have to taste great. Learning to work with rice paper can open up a whole new cooking repertoire to you, including wonderful wonton.

½ small white onion
6 king prawns (jumbo shrimp) in their shells
1 tablespoon cooking sake
300 ml (10 fl oz/1¼ cups) water
3 teaspoons rice bran oil
1 teaspoon cornflour (cornstarch)
1 large (US extra-large) egg
2 pinches of salt, plus extra for rubbing
1 teaspoon sesame oil, plus extra to drizzle
2 sheets of rice paper
½ teaspoon oyster sauce
Slice of lime, to serve

See previous page step-by-step images.

1. Slice the white onion into thin rings. Peel the prawns, retaining the shells, and remove the vein. Rinse the prawns shells thoroughly with water.

2. Over a bowl, rub the prawn meat with the sake and rinse in the same bowl with the measured water. Don't throw away this water.

3. To make the soup base, put the prawn shells and 2 teaspoons of the rice bran oil into a pot over a medium heat. Stir-fry for about 2 minutes until you can smell the seafood aroma. Add the reserved sake water to the pan, cover with a lid, bring to a simmer, then turn down the heat to low and cook for 30 minutes. Strain through a colander but again reserve the liquid. You are building depth of flavour.

4. For the prawn wontons, rub the prawns thoroughly with salt and rinse under running water. This will get rid of any fishy smell. Chop the prawns into quarters and coat them with 1 teaspoon of sesame oil and the cornflour.

5. Meanwhile, crack the egg into a small bowl and beat until the yolk and white are thoroughly combined.
6. Cut the rice paper lengthways into 3 equal pieces. To rehydrate the dry rice paper, wet some kitchen paper towel and place it on a chopping board. Soak each piece of rice paper in warm water (about 40°C/104°F) for 20–30 seconds. When it becomes floppy, remove it from the bowl and shake it gently to get rid of the excess water, then place it on the damp kitchen paper (this will keep the rice paper moist).
7. Place a teaspoon's worth of prawn on the bottom edge of the rice paper. Fold the bottom corner diagonally to the top far corner to form a triangle. Fold each side of that triangle over and diagonally up. Pinch the edges closed. Make a total of 6 of these.
8. Now heat the remaining 1 teaspoon of the rice bran oil in a separate small saucepan and fry the sliced white onion. When it is fragrant, add the prawn soup stock, oyster sauce and salt, then drop in the prawn wontons and let it bubble for 2 minutes.
9. Remove the prawn wontons from the soup with a slotted spoon and set aside in a bowl. Add the beaten egg mixture straight into the stock, and when it puffs and floats to the top, turn off the heat.
10. Pour the soup into bowls and place the wontons in the soup. Top with a twist of lime as desired and a drizzle of sesame oil.

CHEESY CHICKEN IN RICE PAPER

Makes 4

Cheese and chicken make happy bedfellows, and in this recipe you can indulge in both. There is a knack to creating the perfect little triangular morsels, but it doesn't take long to master, and I find creating these parcels almost meditative.

---

200 grams (7 oz) skinless, boneless chicken breast
Salt and pepper, to taste
4 sheets of rice paper
4–6 slices hard cheese, such as Cheddar cheese
1 tablespoon olive oil
Salad leaves, to serve

1. Cut the chicken breasts into very small pieces: the thinner the pieces are, the better they will cook through evenly. Season the chicken pieces with salt and pepper.

2. To rehydrate the dry rice paper, wet some kitchen paper towel and place it on a chopping board. Soak each piece of rice paper in warm water (about 40°C/104°F) for 20–30 seconds. When floppy, remove it from the bowl and shake gently to get rid of the excess water, then place it on the kitchen paper towel.

3. Arrange the rice paper in a diamond shape in front of you. Now make three layers in the middle of the diamond shape, first with a piece of chicken, followed by a slice of cheese and then another layer of chicken.

4. Fold the bottom pointed edge of the rice paper in toward the middle, then fold the left and right sides of the rice paper in. Now roll it up from bottom to top, enclosing the chicken so there are no gaps between it and the rice paper.

5. Heat the olive oil in a frying pan over a low heat, and slowly cook the wrapped chicken breasts for about 5 minutes each on both sides.

6. Garnish with salad leaves on the side.

HANDMADE CRISPY CURRY SAUSAGES

Makes 5

This recipe doesn't use shop-bought sausages but instead shows you how to make your own in moments. By creating the sausage filling, you can add additional flavourings – in this case, the warmth and spice of curry powder and a hint of cheesiness to amplify the salty satisfaction of these crunchy treats.

---

200 grams (7 oz) minced (ground) beef
200 grams (7 oz) minced (ground) pork
1 tablespoon grated Parmesan cheese
1 tablespoon cooking sake
2 teaspoons curry powder
2 teaspoons cornflour (cornstarch)
1 teaspoon salt
1 teaspoon ground nutmeg
1 teaspoon grated garlic
5 sheets of rice paper
1 tablespoon vegetable oil
Tomato ketchup, to serve
Flat leaf parsley, chopped, to serve

See the chapter opener for this recipe's image.

1. Put the minced beef and pork into a bowl and add the Parmesan cheese, sake, curry powder, cornflour, salt, nutmeg and grated garlic. Knead the mixture until everything is combined and sticky, then divide into 5 equal portions. Roll each portion into a sausage shape and set aside.

2. Dip a sheet of rice paper quickly into a bowl of water and unfold it. Now place one of the meat portions across the sheet. Place chopsticks on top to hold the sausage in place and roll the sheet over the mixture to form a tube. Twist both ends to secure the sausage. Repeat the process until you have used all your sheets.

3. Add a little vegetable oil to a frying pan over a low heat. Once it is hot, place the sausage rolls in the pan and cook for about 10 minutes, turning them every so often so they cook evenly.

4. When they are crispy, golden brown all over and cooked through, serve them on a plate with a little ketchup (spicy varieties work well) and a sprinkling of parsley.

STEAMED PRAWN SPRING ROLL

Makes 4

Spring rolls originated in China and initially looked more like flattened folded pancakes. They get their name as they were often made to commemorate the first day of springtime or the spring festival that falls on Chinese New Year. Their golden elongated roll shape echoes the shape of a bar of gold, and so they usher in prosperity. Instead of ordering them from a takeaway, try making these delicious parcels at home with this foolproof recipe.

---

4 sheets of rice paper
12 prawns (shrimp) in their shells
1 tablespoon water
1 teaspoon salt
1 tablespoon cornflour (cornflour)
1 tablespoon cooking sake
20 grams (¾ oz/2 medium) spring onions (scallions)

Sauce
1 teaspoon very finely chopped garlic
1 tablespoon oyster sauce
1 tablespoon Japanese soy sauce
1 teaspoon sugar
½ teaspoon lemon juice
2 tablespoons water

1. Peel the prawns and remove the vein from the back. Place the prawns in a bowl containing the water, salt and cornflour. Rub this mixture over the prawns to rid them of any fishy smell or dirt, then rinse with water. Soak the washed prawns in a shallow bowl with the sake.

2. Trim the roots off the spring onions and slice the stalks into slim discs.

3. To rehydrate the dry rice paper, wet some kitchen paper towel and place it on a chopping board. Soak each piece of rice paper in warm water (about 40°C/104°F) for 20–30 seconds. When it becomes floppy, remove from the bowl and shake gently to get rid of the excess water, then place it on the kitchen paper towel.

4. Arrange the rehydrated rice paper in a diamond shape in front of you and place some chopped spring onions and 3 prawns in the middle.

5. Now fold the bottom point of the rice paper toward the middle, followed by the left and right sides of the rice paper. Roll the whole thing up from the bottom to top, being careful to trap as little air as possible.

6. Once you have formed 4 rolls, place a piece of parchment (baking) paper on a plate, place the rolls on top and steam in a steamer for 5 minutes.

7. Meanwhile, make the sauce: add the garlic, oyster sauce, Japanese soy sauce, sugar, lemon juice and water to a small frying pan over a low heat and bring them to a simmer. Take care not to overheat it to preserve the soy sauce flavour.

8. Transfer the rolls from the steamer to a small plate and put the sauce in a dipping bowl to enjoy.

SWEET POTATO CAKES

Makes 10

Sweet potato is not native to Japan but made its way there from Central South America, via the Philippines and China, several hundred years ago. It is now a popular cooking ingredient. The caramelized sweetness of these orange-fleshed vegetables delivers a highly nutritious hit, with just one veggie containing your daily recommended vitamin A quota. This dish is vegetarian, but you can switch the dairy milk used here for a vegan alternative if desired.

---

1 medium sweet potato
140 grams (5 oz/½ cup) azuki bean paste
Milk, as required
5 sheets of rice paper
1 packet sesame seeds
2 teaspoons sesame oil

1. If you like a rustic mash, you can leave the peel on, but if you prefer a smoother texture, peel the sweet potato. With or without the peel, cut the sweet potato into bite-sized pieces and soak them in water for about 15 minutes.

2. Drain the water and cover loosely with cling film (plastic wrap). Cook the sweet potato in a microwave oven (600W) for about 5 minutes. Alternatively, put it in a steamer basket over a saucepan of simmering water and steam for 10–15 minutes until softened.

3. Once soft, mash the sweet potato in a bowl with a fork. If the sweet potato needs a little moisture to come together, add a little splash of milk to help.

4. Lay out 5 smallish pieces of cling film and mound an equal amount of the mashed sweet potato on top of each piece of cling film and spread it into a circular shape. Divide the azuki bean paste into 5 equal portions and place on top of each

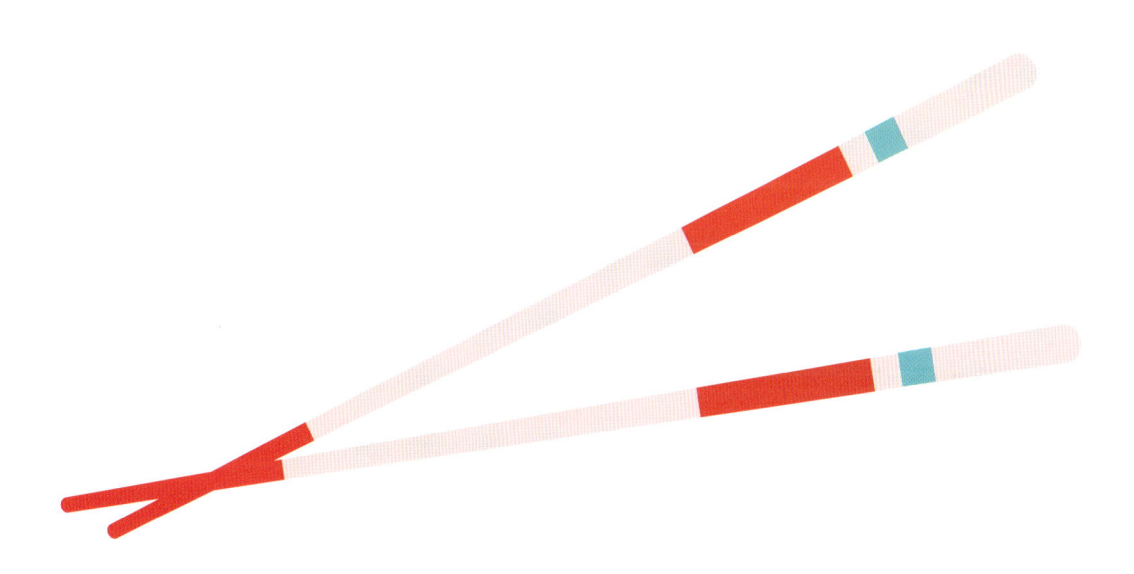

circle. Now bring up the ends of the cling film to enfold the azuki bean paste in the centre of the sweet potato, forming a ball. Wrap each ball up in cling film and squeeze the sides lightly to form a square shape. Gently remove the cling film.

5. Cut each sheet of rice paper in half with scissors. Soak both halves in water for 1 minute to soften. Make sure they don't touch together and stick at this stage.

6. Use 2 halves of rice paper per dumpling. Place the first softened half-sheet of rice paper in the palm of your hand. Now place a sweet potato square on top and wrap the rice paper round it. Place the other sheet of rice paper over the dumpling and wrap it up. Gently roll the wrapped balls and lightly flatten into a cake shape. Put the dumpling cake on a shallow plate covered in sesame seeds and turn it around to evenly coat in the seeds.

7. Add a little sesame oil to a frying pan over a medium heat. When it's hot, arrange the sesame-covered dumplings in the pan. Fry for about 5 minutes on each side until golden brown.

DUCK PANCAKES

Makes 4

Duck is often associated with high-end French cuisine, but in Asia it is a favoured poultry as it has a unique flavour, is easy to prepare and is very versatile. The key is rendering off the fatty skin by searing it, skin side down, in a hot pan. Once you have perfected cooking duck, you can easily create your own duck pancakes at home.

---

1 whole cucumber
3 spring onions (scallions)
200 grams (7 oz) boneless duck breast with its skin
Pinch of salt and pepper
½ teaspoon very finely chopped garlic
¼ teaspoon Chinese five-spice powder
1 teaspoon olive oil
4 sheets of rice paper
1 tablespoon temanjen (sweet bean paste) or hoisin sauce

1. Cut off the ends of the cucumber, then cut it in half lengthways and slice into thin strips. Trim the roots of the spring onions and cut the stalks in half lengthways, then also cut them into thin strips. Place in a bowl of water for about 5 minutes and drain.

2. Coat the duck breast with salt and pepper, garlic and five spice powder, rubbing it all over the skin and underside.

3. Add the olive oil to a frying pan over a medium heat. Once hot, place the duck breast skin side down. Press down with a spatula and wipe off excess oil with kitchen paper towel while cooking for about 3 minutes until nicely browned.

4. Turn the breast over and reduce the heat to low. Now cook for about 5 minutes until the duck breast is cooked through, then remove from the heat. Allow it to cool, then slice thinly.

5. Rapidly dip the rice paper into warm water at about 40°C (104°F) for 20–30 seconds each, then place on a chopping board, arranging them in a diamond shape.

6. Place the duck slices, cucumber, spring onion, and sweet bean paste on top of each sheet of rice paper. Now fold up the bottom of the rice paper, then fold in the left and right sides of the rice paper. Finish by rolling the sheet from bottom to top.
7. Serve whole or cut in half, arrange on a plate and you're done.

CLASSIC PRAWN SPRING ROLLS

Makes 4

These classic little rolls are superlight and a perennial favourite, requiring very few ingredients. Wrapped in rice paper that has been lightly soaked to rehydrate, the translucent outer layer reveals the fresh ingredients within, for a sumptuous summer time meal.

4 peeled prawns (shrimp)
100 grams (3½ oz/1 cup) beansprouts
½ a whole cucumber, cut lengthways
2 cos lettuce leaves
4 sheets of rice paper
500 ml (17 fl oz/2 cups) water
1 teaspoon salt
1 tablespoon sweet chilli sauce (optional)
1 teaspoon temanjen (sweet bean paste; optional)
1 teaspoon sesame oil (optional)

1. Bring a saucepan of salted water to a boil over a high heat. Add the beansprouts and cook briefly before removing with a slotted spoon or sieve. Next, tip the prawns into the pan and simmer for about 1½ minutes before straining.

2. Set the prawns aside to cool. Once cooled, using a sharp knife, cut them down the back into halves.

3. Remove the end of the cucumber half and thinly slice diagonally. Tear the lettuce leaves into bite-sized pieces.

4. Wet the rice paper with water and spread it out on a wrung-out cloth. Place one quarter of the beansprouts on top. Follow with the two halved prawns per sheet, then cucumber slices and lettuce leaves. Roll up from the bottom. Two thirds of the way up, fold the left and right sides back in to the centre, and continue rolling tightly to complete the spring rolls.

5. Cut into bite-sized pieces and serve on a plate with sweet chilli sauce. Alternatively, mix the *temanjen* with the sesame oil and serve with the rolls.

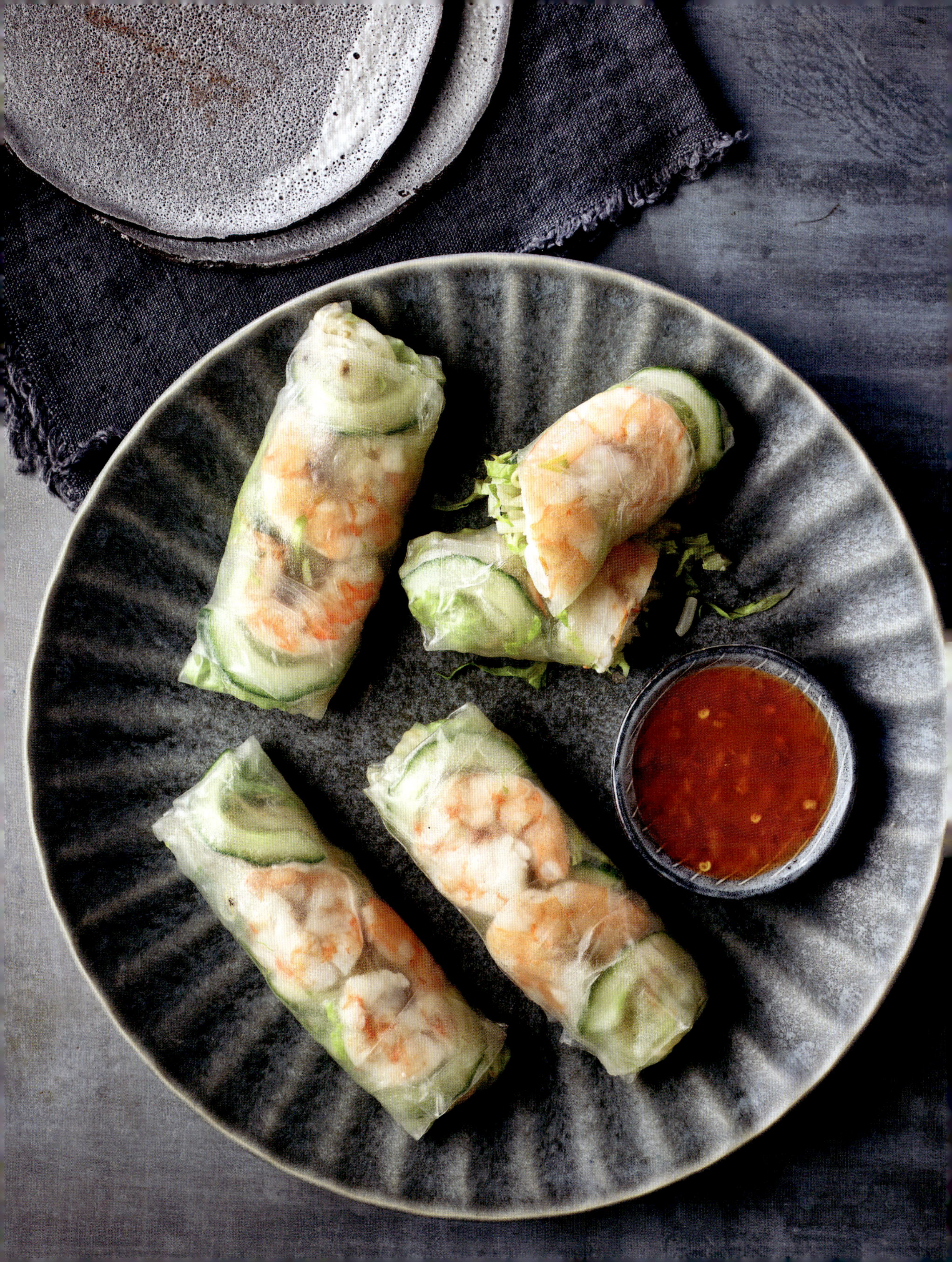

INDEX

A

anchovy 148
Aromatic rice soup 70
asparagus 42
aubergine (eggplant) 42, 108
auki bean paste 164
avocado 28, 46, 122
Avocado fried rice 122
azuki bean paste 116

B

bacon 89
bamboo shoots 38
basil 52
beansprouts 44, 50, 52, 54, 168
beef 32, 44, 52, 132, 161
Beef rice noodles 52
bell pepper 56, 60, 92, 101, 108, 143
Bibimbap don 44
biscuits 155
bonito flakes 70, 122, 136, 146
breadcrumbs 34
bream, sea 72
Buttered sardine rice 96

C

cabbage
   Chinese (napa) 38, 110
   Savoy 134, 152
carrot 38, 44, 89, 108, 152
cheese (hard) 66, 106, 112, 114, 154, 160, 161
Cheese onigiri 66
Cheesy chicken in rice paper 160
Cheesy rice flour muffins 112
Chestnut rice 100
chestnuts 100
chicken 36, 50, 60, 90, 92, 98, 143, 160
Chicken pho 50
Chicken rice with tomato 90
chilli
   flakes 124
   oil 26, 63,
   paste 44, 132
   pepper strands 63
   powder 63, 152
   sauce 36, 168
chipolatas 122
chives 34, 101, 132
   Chinese 54, 152
chocolate 115
chocolate chips 115, 118
Chuukadon 38
Classic Chinese fried rice 125
Classic prawn spring rolls 168
Coconut chicken rice 143
Coconut mango rice 84

coconut
  milk *60, 84, 94, 143*
  oil *115*
  sugar *54,*
coriander (cilantro) 50, 52, 101, 143
Corn curry fried rice *124*
courgette (zucchini) 56, 108
cream cheese 112, 155
cucumber 166, 168

D

daikon (mooli) 44, 54
Dashi stock *70, 72*
Donburi *31*
Double eggs gohan *24*
dressings 63, 98
duck 166
Duck pancakes *166*

E

Easy rice porridge *71*
Egg soup fried rice *137*
eggs 20, 24, 25, 26, 28, 34, 36, 40, 42, 44, 54, 58, 68, 108, 112, 115, 118, 125, 126, 128, 130, 132, 136, 137, 158
  quail's *38*
Eggy butter rice *25*

F

fish sauce 50, 52, 54, 152
Fluffy rice flour pancakes *104*
Fragrant dashi rice with fish *72*
frankfurter (sausage) 93
Fried beef with sunny side up egg *132*
fried rice 121

G

garlic 25, 44, 46, 52, 88, 89, 93, 110, 128, 134, 137, 143, 152, 161, 162, 166
Garlic sausage rice *93*
garnishes 50, 52
Giant onigiri sandwich *68*
ginger 26, 44, 50, 52, 82, 94, 98, 126, 132, 140, 143, 146
  pickled *26, 32*
Ginger octopus rice *140*
gochujang (Korean chilli paste) 44, 132
Gyudon *32*

H

Handmade crispy curry sausages *161*
Healthy breakfast rice *149*
hoisin sauce 166

I

ikura (salmon roe) 24

J

Jambala rice *92*
japonica rice 20, 24, 26, 28, 32, 34, 36, 38, 40, 42, 44, 46, 66, 68, 70, 71, 72, 74, 76, 78, 82, 92, 93, 98, 101, 140, 142, 144, 146, 148

K

Kake gohan *19, 26*
kale 136
Katsu don *34*
kelp 40, 70, 76, 144
kimchi 20, 62, 130
Kimchi tamago gohan *20*

kombu (kelp) 70
Korean seaweed 20

L

leek 146
lettuce 68, 146, 154, 168
lotus root 60

M

mackerel 136
Mackerel fried rice 136
mangetout (snow pea) 38
mango 84
marinades 24, 46
Matcha paper-wrapped cheesecake 155
mayonnaise 68, 78, 154
mint 50
mirin 24, 32, 34, 36, 40, 42, 46, 66, 72, 109, 140, 146, 149,
Miso milk kimchi pho 62
miso paste 62, 146
mitsuba (Japanese parsley) 72
mizuna 76
Mizuna & salmon rice tea 76
mushroom
    button 90
    enoki 124, 152
    oyster 148
    shimeji 148
    shiitake 42, 88, 96, 148
    wood ear 38
Mushroom & anchovy rice 148
mussels 82
Mussels & wasabi with roasted green tea 82
myoga 26

N

No-fall sticky rice 88
noodles, rice 49
    flat rice 50, 52, 54, 58, 60, 62, 63
    vermicelli 56

O

oba 26
octopus (tentacles) 140
olive oil 40, 60, 88, 89, 92, 104, 106, 111, 114, 122, 124, 128, 132, 134, 136, 137, 148, 160,166
Omusubi (rice balls) 63
Onigiri 65
onion
    spring 20, 26, 36, 38, 46, 50, 58, 60, 62, 63, 80, 82, 88, 96, 98, 124, 125, 126, 127, 128, 130, 132, 134, 137, 162, 166
    white 32, 34, 36, 56, 58, 60, 78, 89, 92, 101, 106, 132, 143, 158
Oyakodon 36
oyster saucer 56, 152, 158, 162

P

Pad Thai 54
pak choi (bok choy) 58
parsley 72, 92, 142, 161
pepperoni 106
Pho with pork & courgette curry 56
Pizza toppings 106
pork 34, 38, 56, 58, 63, 88, 110, 130, 137, 152, 161
Pork and kimchi fried rice 130
Pork pho Chinese 58
prawn (shrimp) 42, 54, 74, 108, 158, 162, 168
Prawn wonton soup 157–8
Protein bowl tamori don 26
pumpkin 60

INDEX

R

rice, essential info (see also below for ingredients; recipes)
  benefits of 13
  cooking, how to 14–16, 87
    & storing leftovers 16
  flour 12, 13, 17, 103
  in Japanese culture 6–9
  in Japanese meals 8
  noodles, types of 17
    dishes suited to 17
  types of 10–11
    brown 8, 11
    how to cook 14
    glutinous 10
    cooking 15
    haiga-mai 12
    hatsuga-genmai (GABA) 11–12
    Indica 10
    Japonica 10
    white 'Uruchi-mai' 10–11
    jasmine (Thai) 11
    Javanica 10
    mochigome 12
    musenmai 12
    non-glutinous 10
    onigiri 10
    purple 13
    shichibu-zuki 12
    stir-frying, best for 11
    sushi 8, 10
    white 8
    zakkoku (kokumotsu) 13
  vitamins in 13

rice, ingredients, see also noodles; Thai (jasmine); wine
  basmati 143
  bran oil 56, 112, 152, 158
  brown 149
  flour 103
  paper 151, 152, 154, 155, 158, 160, 161, 162, 164, 166, 168
  sticky (glutinous) 84, 88, 116
  vinegar 126

rice, recipes
  Rice flour and yogurt nanna bread 114
  Rice flour brownies 115
  Rice flour chocolate chip cookies 118
  Rice flour gyoza 110
  Rice flour pizza 106
  Rice flour tempura 108
rocket (angula) 76
rum 115

S

sake (rice wine) 12, 24, 32, 34, 36, 38, 40, 44, 50, 52, 58, 88, 92, 98, 100, 110, 126, 128, 132, 140, 142, 148, 158, 161, 162
salmon 76, 80, 128, 146, 154
Salmon & avocado paper roll 154
Salmon & flavoured leek lettuce bowl 146
Salmon with green tea chazuke 80
Salted salmon garlic fried rice 128
sardine 96
sauces 32, 34, 36, 42, 54, 56, 63, 72, 109, 153, 162
Scalloped fried rice with garlic and butter 134
scallops 134
Sea chicken mayo onigiri 78
seafood, mixed 101, 126
Seafood rice 101
Seafood Tianjin rice in a sauce 126
seaweed 80, 82
  nori 28, 68, 74, 78
  Korean 22, 44
  wakame 149
Sesame sauce 72

INDEX 173

sesame
   oil 20, 38, 44, 46, 63, 66, 76, 98, 104, 110, 125, 126, 130, 132, 137, 146, 149, 152, 158, 164, 168
   seed 46, 72, 76, 80, 84, 88, 93, 100, 146, 148, 164
shichimi 36, 66
shiso (perilla) 26, 74
Shredded chicken & spring onion rice 98
shrimp, dried 54
Simple coconut rice 94
Spicy pho 63
spinach 40, 44
Spring-onion dressing 98
Steamed prawn spring roll 162
stock 52, 70
store cupboard basics 17
Store cupboard curry 89
strawberies 116, 155
Strawberries & cream mochi 116
sweet potato 144, 164
Sweet potato butter rice 144
Sweet potato cakes 164
sweetcorn 89, 92, 101, 124, 142
Sweetcorn butter rice 142

T

tahini (sesame paste) 63
takikomi gohan hotate rice 139
Tamakake gohan 20
tamarind paste 54
tea
   green 80, 82
   leaves 7
   sencha 70
temanjen (sweet bean paste) 166, 168
Tempura batter 42
Tempura dipping sauce 109
Tempura onigiri 74
Tendon 42

tenmenjiang (sweet bean sauce) 63
Thai green curry paste 60
Thai green curry pho noodles 60
Thai (jasmine) rice 89, 90, 94, 96, 98, 122, 124, 125, 126, 128, 130, 132, 134, 136, 137, 146, 148
Thai/Vietnamese-style spring rolls 152
tofu 26, 40, 54, 152
Tofu don 40
tograshi 36
tomatoes 90, 106
tuna 28, 46, 68, 78
Tuna poke 46

W

wasabi 24, 28, 46, 72, 82, 154
Wasabi-flavoured avocado & egg rice 28
Wrappers 111

Y

yogurt 114
yuzu pepper 122

Z

zha cai 58, 63

SUPPLIERS

UK SUPPLIERS

CS Mart – Japanese Supermarket
18 Queensway, London, W2 3RX

Ikkyu Conveni
102 Ladbroke Grove, London, W11 1PY

Japan Centre Ichiba
0220 Relay Square Westfield, London, W12 7HB

WASO: Online Japanese Supermarket
waso.tokyo

Oseyo Hammersmith
Unit 5b, 6 Hammersmith Broadway, London, W6 9YD

Oseyo Soho
73-75 Charing Cross Rd, London, WC2H 0BF

Rice Wine
82 Brewer St, London, W1F 9UA

US SUPPLIERS

Just Asian Food
justasianfood.com
Includes a category for Japanese foods such as noodles, seasonings, sauces and soup bases.

Just Hungry
justhungry.com
Website dedicated to Japanese recipes that has links to Japanese grocery stores in the United States and its territories.

Kokoro Care
kokorocares.com/collections/market-michi-no-eki
Supplies natural products made in Japan without chemicals, from dashi packets to seasonings and noodles, as well as care packages fill with artisan Japanese food; they will delivery worldwide but have a minimum order to do so.

Umami Insider
umami-insider.store
Specialty store supplying high-quality ingredients from Japan, including storecupboard staples such as seaweed, seasonings such as shichimi togarashi, and vegetables such as umeboshi and dried shiitake.

Yamibuy
yamibuy.com
Extensive grocery range of Japanese, Korean and Chinese products and ingredients.

ABOUT THE AUTHOR

I chose to become a chef because I take great pleasure in cooking, enjoying exquisite meals, and seeing the happiness that comes when people gather and share laughter over food. I genuinely believe that food has the ability to bring people together, creating joy.

In our fast-paced world, many individuals avoid cooking because of their busy lives. Yet, cooking can serve as a therapeutic and creative outlet that doesn't need to consume a lot of time.

Through this book, I aim to encourage more people to appreciate the art of cooking just as much as they enjoy eating.

Happy cooking!

Makiko Sano

CREDITS

With kind thanks to Simon Smith Photography simonsmithphotography.co.uk, Morag Farquhar and Prop Supply Co for props, and Becks Wilkinson for food styling.

The publishers would also like to thank the following sources for their kind permission to reproduce the pictures in this book.

Alamy 6 CPA Media Pte Ltd / 7 Panther Media GmbH / 11l Yannawit Dhammasaro / 11r Cromo Digital / 12 Horst Friedrichs / 13 Tetiana Vitsenko / 14 Aycan Aykan / 15 Brent Hofacker
Shutterstock 8 Ao Nori / 17 Michelle Lee Photography
Unsplash 9 Alexander Schimmeck / 10 Andrey Câmara
Freepik 153, 165 studiogstock